To Crewe

a

THE SOUL OF WIT

THE SOUL OF WIT

A CHOICE OF

ENGLISH VERSE EPIGRAMS

MADE BY

GEORGE ROSTREVOR HAMILTON

LONDON
WILLIAM HEINEMANN, LTD.
1924

Printed in Great Britain
at The Westminster Press
Harrow Road
London, W.9

Praise not the epigram, nor censure it,
Merely for clever malice or smart wit :
Look in this volume ; in it you shall see
Not one but every mood's epitome.

INTRODUCTION

THOUSANDS of bad and indifferent epigrams have been written in English verse. Hundreds of these have been printed and reprinted with conservative zeal in miscellanies of poetry and in epigram collections. It is not to be wondered at that readers have become tired, and that interest has flagged. Of really good epigrams, if you exclude translations from the Greek Anthology,* I doubt whether a thousand have been written and have survived.

A wrong tradition has grown up, particularly in the last fifty years. The work of the past has been over-praised, and it has been suggested that epigrammatic art, after a slow decline, is now moribund. It is true that the seventeenth century produced epitaphs of astonishing beauty, the eighteenth produced inimitable examples of urbane wit, the earlier nineteenth produced —Landor. But the common run of

* Much fine work continues to be done in verse translation from the Greek. It is a pleasure to be able to include in this book a few, for instance, of the many admirable versions by Dr. A. J. Butler and Dr. Walter Leaf. They find place here, not as translations of fine Greek epigrams, but rather as fine English epigrams.

seventeenth-century epigram was clumsy, obscene and dull : the common run of eighteenth-century epigram was accomplished and dull : the common run of the early nineteenth facetious and dull. Throughout, a vast amount of rubbish—poor in humour, poor in taste—was written. In the present century, and in the latter half of the nineteenth, there have been fewer epigrams. This, however, is not a bad economy, for there have been fewer to deplore. The important thing is that the output of good work has been steady, although little noticed.*

My book would have small excuse for its existence, if it were not something of a challenge. In compiling it, I have followed my own personal taste, believing this, with all its risks, to be the right method. I am not so foolish as to suppose that any one reader will entirely agree with me—what man, with convictions, is ever completely satisfied by any anthology (even by his own) ? Among my own friends whose opinions I respect, I have found no little disagreement. What of it ? I must hope for

* Books of epigrams have been scarce, but Sir William Watson's early book (1884) would have been remarkable in any time. He stands high among English epigrammatists, and the twelve poems I have chosen for this volume are only specimens of his fine achievement.

the best. As a quatrain in *Wit's Recreations* (1640) forcibly puts it :

Who seeks to please all men each way,
  And not himself offend,
He may begin to work to-day,
  But God knows when he'll end.

It can fairly be said that no existing collection of epigrams gives sufficient space to serious and imaginative wit. The humorous and satirical type, established by Martial, is still commonly regarded as the epigram proper. Yet surely it is absurd to adhere slavishly to old definitions. The meaning of the word epigram is determined by the practice of English writers, and is elastic enough to change with that practice. Mr. T. S. Eliot has very truly said that " what happens when a new work of art is created is something that happens simultaneously to all the works of art which preceded it."[*] So, when Landor wrote, a stir went through the polite ranks of the eighteenth-century wits, and the art of epigram was enlarged. Within it, the short poem of concise, imaginative wit was given a new and a definite place.

It is useless, I believe, to attempt any precise definition of epigram. A trinity of formal characteristics may, however, be

[*] Essay on " Tradition and the Individual Talent " in *The Sacred Wood*, p. 44 (Methuen & Co., Ltd.).

noticed. *First*, and most obvious, is brevity, which is the soul of wit—of wit, not quite of humour, for humour is often expansive. Even as to brevity no exact measure can be laid down. I have taken twelve lines, in not more than two clearly-defined stanzas, as the extreme limit of length, but the limit is quite arbitrary. *Secondly*, there are the qualities of conciseness and finality. The typical epigram is complete in itself. Even if it opens up a long view, it is a view held within a clear-cut frame. The following quatrain by Ambrose Philips I have not considered to be an epigram :—

In Answer to the Question, What is Thought?
The hermit's solace in his cell,
The fire that warms the poet's brain,
The lover's heaven, or his hell,
The madman's sport, the wise man's pain.

It is a charming fragment, concise indeed, but not unified, not final.

Again I exclude Browning's well-known lines :—

Round the cape of a sudden came the sea,
And the sun look'd over the mountain's rim :
And straight was a path of gold for him,
And the need of a world of men for me.

Here the sketch of scene and mood is all suggestion. It is unfixed, it flashes and fades. The beginning suggests that it was not the beginning, and at the end no end comes into sight.

The *third* characteristic of the epigram is a quality—or rather a group of qualities—which may be called rhetorical. The epigram is speech rather than song. It has the calculation of rhetoric rather than the abandonment of lyric. It has to make a point in a few words : it delights in antithesis, in balance, in neat allusion, in prepared climax : it considers every word, distributing the weight of sound, the emphasis of accent, so that every word may tell and the force be concentrated, or at least maintained, at the close.

Between pure rhetoric and pure lyric there are, of course, many degrees. A lyrical poem is often epigrammatic, and it is impossible, sometimes, to say with authority whether an epigrammatic poem is an epigram. It is a question for individual judgment. I have not been able to find complete consistency in any collection, and do not claim it for mine : but I think I have been strict enough to satisfy a tradition which, in this respect, appears reasonable enough. One of the difficult poets to deal with is Herrick. His verses which bear the name of epigram deserve no consideration : they are wretched in quality, as well as unpleasant. But how are his charming diminutive poems to be classed ? Most are clearly lyrics or lyrical snatches, but some are certainly epigrams : others, though epigrammatic in idea, seem to be too lyrical in feeling and execution to be admitted ; they lack the epigrammatic finish. To give an example, I have not hesitated to print the quatrain, *Upon a Gentlewoman with a Sweet Voice* (p. 79) ; on the other hand I have excluded the lines *Upon Julia's Voice*, which are still more entrancing :—

So smooth, so sweet, so silv'ry is thy
    voice,
As, could they hear, the Damn'd would
    make no noise,
But listen to thee (walking in thy chamber)
Melting melodious words to Lutes of
    Amber.

Once or twice I have been glad to have precedent for the inclusion of a poem only doubtfully to be called an epigram. One such poem is that by Richard Graves, *Venus Genetrix, Mrs. W——n.* 1760 (p. 59). In this case the precedent was first set by the author himself, who printed the lines in his anthology, *The Festoon*. Whether strictly an epigram or not, the poem deserves a fame it has never won : it has a formal yet tender loveliness, not common in eighteenth-century verse, yet found in that century alone.

I have not always taken advantage of precedent. For example, Landor's most widely-known poem, *Rose Aylmer*, has been counted an epigram, but it is not among the twenty-seven Landor poems which I have selected. To me it is essentially a lyric. Moreover, I will confess that its exclusion has not cost me a night without sleep. Its perfection of form is typical of the whole artist ; its too measured emotion is not typical of the whole man. *Rose Aylmer*, and the lines, " I strove with none " (p. 108), have been given undue pre-eminence in Landor's work : they have distracted attention from many other epigrams of first-class excellence, some of which have, for me at least, a finer emotional quality. Consider—to name only four—*Ianthe's Question* (p. 94), *The Demand* (p. 94), *The Tear Denied* (p. 97), *Retirement* (p. 108).

The omission of *Rose Aylmer* leads me to mention certain other omissions. The ungallant epigram I have, for the most part, ignored. I cannot express too strongly my distaste for such a couplet as Dryden's

Here lies my wife ! Here let her lie !
Now she's at rest, and so am I.

The humour is very ordinary, the tone is

insolent, and the shaping, while neat and terse, is not beyond the smartness of a Sixth Form scholarship boy. The rhyme would never have been preserved as a model of wit, but for the great name of Dryden, and but for a taste which, I believe, we have outgrown, if we would but candidly confess it. This taste has delighted in epigrams on women with bought or dyed hair, women with detachable eyebrows, squinting poetesses, etc., etc. How mean and stale they are! They cannot be redeemed by mere smartness, or mere versifying skill. Even the exquisite Matthew Prior, whose touch in epigram is so admirably light, cannot commend them. He has been among the worst of offenders.

Dryden's is not the only name that has given undeserved life to an epigram. I have tried, in my selection, not to be a respecter of persons. Some of the great poets have been inferior epigrammatists, and the best of the epigrammatists—even Prior and Landor—have not infrequently written mediocre epigrams. It is no honour to a fine poet to snatch at some trifle of his in order that he may be represented,—to print Matthew Arnold's *Persistency of Poetry*, with its bad last line, or his clumsily expressed *Caution to Poets*, or, again, Tennyson's rather silly effusion, *To Christopher*

North. Again, it seems to me that it would be impossible to do Coleridge any service by giving more than one or two of his *jeux d'esprit.* Most of them are lamentable, and even some which are really clever—*Job's Luck* and *Cologne*—are spoiled by an air of jaunty self-satisfaction, a distressing species of vulgarity. It is a pity that this should infect *Cologne*, the last five lines of which are excellent—

> Ye Nymphs that reign o'er sewers and
>   sinks,
> The River Rhine, it is well known,
> Doth wash your city of Cologne ;
> But tell me, Nymphs, what power divine
> Shall henceforth wash the river Rhine ?

There is nothing more ruinous to an epigram than the tone which seems to say, Look, how gay and clever I am! This sprightly tone was peculiarly common in the early nineteenth century, and, to me at least, its effect is most irritating. The pun was greatly in fashion ; it may be that the suggestion of smug self-gratulation is difficult to avoid in the punning type of humour, especially when the metre chosen is the anapaestic jingle beloved of Tom Moore. However it may be, the suggestion is there. What are we to say of the laborious ingenuity of James Smith (of the *Rejected Addresses*), when he makes a father say to his daughter, who has asked him for money :—

> Dear Bell, to gain money, sure, silence is best,
> For dumb Bells are fittest to open the chest.*

Can we share the author's satisfaction ? Rather, with Platonic firmness, will we exclude James Smith, along with Theodore Hook and others, from our city. Even the amiable Tom Hood we will barely admit. He was a true master of punning, and punning is an art not to be despised : but his humour was of the genial, expansive kind, whose soul is not brevity. Epigram gave no room for his high spirits ; he was at his best when he could rain blow after blow upon the reader, a succession of puns breaking all resistance.

Some epigrams deserve to be remembered for their anecdotal value rather than for their own merit. Among these I am inclined to put the Earl of Rochester's quatrain on King Charles II :—

> Here lies our sovereign Lord the King,
> Whose word no man relies on,
> Who never said a foolish thing
> Nor ever did a wise one.

* A favourite of the anthologists. Even Dodd (*The Epigrammatists*, 1870), who does not think too well of the punning epigram, calls it " one of the best " of its class.

Historically, these lines may be very apt, but they appear to me to be only moderately witty and well-turned, and to be outshone by the King's retort—his words were his own, but his acts were the acts of his ministers. Another well-known quatrain, which hardly deserves its fame, is that on Dr. Fell, one time Dean of Christ Church, Oxford :—

I do not love thee, Doctor Fell ;
The reason why I cannot tell.
But this I'm sure I know full well,
I do not love thee, Doctor Fell.

I had an affection for this often-quoted trifle before I learnt its origin. It is by Thomas Brown (d. 1704), from an epigram by Martial : the story goes that Thomas Brown was in imminent danger of being sent down from Oxford ; "but Tom, with a very submissive epistle, begging pardon, so pleas'd the dean that he was minded to forgive him, upon this condition, viz., that he should translate this epigram out of *Martial* extempore :

Non amo te, Zabidi, nec possum dicere
    quare ;
Hoc tantum possum dicere, nom amo
    Te."*

* *Thomas Brown's Works*, 9th edition, 1760 :
Vol. IV, p. 99.

Tom instantly replied with his quatrain. In not withdrawing the pardon, Dr. Fell may perhaps have won Tom's love : he deserved to.

Most of the epigrams I have mentioned belong to the seventeenth and nineteenth centuries. I will now turn to two of the eighteenth century, both well known, which, after some slight hesitation, I have decided to omit. The first is by Goldsmith, imitated from the Spanish :—

On a Beautiful Youth Struck Blind with Lightning

Sure, 'twas by Providence design'd,
　Rather in pity, than in hate,
That he should be, like Cupid, blind,
　To save him from Narcissus' fate.

This is a well-made epigram, beautifully phrased, but the subject is not one for the play of light fancy. It is beside the point that the verse may have no reference to any actual youth who was blinded, for poetry has to do with imaginative, not with historical, fact : the tragedy of the blind young man is presented as a fact to the imagination, and around it—with unintentional cruelty—a pretty fancy is woven.

The other epigram I have referred to is Dr. Doddridge's *Dum Vivimus, Vivamus* :—

" Live, while you live "—the Epicure
    would say,
" And seize the pleasures of the present
    day."
" Live, while you live," the sacred
    Preacher cries,
" And give to God each moment as it
    flies."
Lord, in my views let both united be ;
I live in pleasure, when I live to Thee.

My hesitation here was caused by Dr.
Johnson having called this " one of the
finest epigrams in the English language."
Despite all my reverence for Dr. Johnson,
I rebel at this judgment. The thought seems
commonplace, and the form is marked by
that exaggerated balance which was one
of the literary dangers of the period. It
suggests nothing so much as the syllogism
of formal logic, and cries out to be parodied ;
in the first couplet the Major Premise would
say that all men are mortal, in the second
the Minor would cry that Socrates was a
man, in the third the Pupil would unite
them in his great conclusion—the mortality
of Socrates.

Unfortunately there are very few parodies
in epigram, apart from the amusing bur-
lesque lines (p. 71) which Dr. Johnson
himself wrote. If there were sufficient to

form a group in my anthology, a couplet by Mr. J. C. Squire would find honourable place. It was suggested to him one evening that there ought to be an epigram on Einstein as a companion to Pope's on Newton :—

> Nature, and Nature's laws, lay hid in night :
> God said, *Let Newton be !* and all was light.

In the good old fashion he called for pencil and paper (but it should have been a diamond pencil and a glass of the Aristotelian Society), and inscribed as follows :—

> It did not last : the Devil, howling *Ho !*
> *Let Einstein be !* restored the status quo.*

Enough has been said about omissions, and there is little further I need to say. In making this collection, my leading desire has been to choose the best epigrams, whoever may have written them. Not all the authors are good poets, not all are good epigrammatists : it is the epigram that

---

* This may possibly recall Pope's own parody—

Here lies Lord Coningsby ; be civil.
The rest God knows, perhaps the Devil.

The model of this was Hercules Stroza's Latin epitaph—

Joannes jacet hic Mirandola ; caetera norunt
Et Tagus, et Ganges, forsan et Antipodes.

matters. A surprising number of indifferent authors have written one or two good epigrams, and, more particularly, good epitaphs. It is with a shock of pleasure that one finds poems like Thomas Bancroft's *On William Holorenshaw, the Mathematician* (p. 106), Samuel Sheppard's *Epitaph on a Virgin dying for Love* (p. 140), Emanuel Collins' *Epitaph on Mistress Rowland* (p. 137). The Englishman, if he is ever a poet, is so in the face of death.

Some of the best things in this book will, indeed, be found among the epitaphs—a good many anonymous. The last Section is wholly devoted to them, but some have been placed in other Sections, where they seemed naturally to belong. In my arrangement of the book I have not followed any rigid divisions. My grouping has been done, for the most part, according to affinity, sometimes superficial, sometimes internal, but the fact that only epigrams of a certain length can be fitted together on a page has been a difficulty. Nevertheless, the epigrams of each Section will, I hope, be found to cohere sufficiently : if they do, then it is of little moment that the headings— " Mainly Humorous and Satirical," etc.— fit them rather loosely.

This and other matters must be left to the eye of the reader. If his eye be unprejudiced, he will, I hope, get a fresh view of the English epigram, and moreover recognise that it did not die in the nineteenth century, but is alive to-day, and may, if he will encourage it, be more alive to-morrow.

GEORGE R. HAMILTON.

September, 1924.

ACKNOWLEDGMENTS

M Y very special thanks are due to Mrs. Patmore and to Mr. Wilfrid Meynell for permission to print an unpublished epigram (p. 113) by Coventry Patmore ; to Mr. J. C. Squire for six unpublished epigrams (pp. 11, 18 (2), 40, 79 and 86), and for generous help and encouragement ; and to Mr. Iolo Williams, for an introduction to several books, and in particular to John Hanway's beautiful epitaph (p. 136) ; the epitaph on *Peter Robinson* (p. 27) I heard from Mr. Wilfrid Meynell, and the Nursery Rhyme which I call *History* (p. 7), from Sir George Collier ; the *Worcestershire epitaph* (p. 100) was found by the late A. Clutton-Brock, and reached me through Mr. A. L. Irvine ; the *Impromptu in a Kirk Gallery* (p. 19) I owe to oral tradition. The lines were written by my maternal grandfather and seem to me worth preserving.

I am glad to thank the many authors and publishers who have given me permission to use copyright lines : Mr. Martin Armstrong (and Mr. Martin Secker) ; Mr. Herbert Asquith (and Messrs. Sidgwick & Jackson) ; Dr. F. P. Barnard (and the Oxford University Press) ; Mr. Hilaire Belloc (and Messrs. Duckworth & Co.) ; Mr. A. C. Benson (and Mr. John Murray) ; Dr. Robert Bridges (and Mr. John Murray) ; Dr. A .J. Butler (and Mr. B. H. Blackwell) ; Mr. G. K. Chesterton (and Messrs. J. M. Dent & Sons, Ltd.) ; Mrs. Frances Cornford (and Mr. Harold Monro) ; Miss Adelaide

Crapsey (and Mr. Alfred A. Knopf); the
Marquess Curzon of Kedleston (and Mr. John
Lane); Mr. Charles Dalmon, for two epigrams
(for one of which, " On Trout leaping in the
Arun," from *A Poor Man's Riches*, acknowledg-
ment is also due to Messrs. Methuen & Co.);
Mr. E. L. Davison; Mr. Walter de la Mare
(with Messrs. Constable & Co. and Messrs.
Selwyn & Blount, the former for " Napoleon,"
and the epitaph, " Here lies a most beautiful
lady," from *Poems*, the latter for three epitaphs
from *Ding Dong Bell*); Mr. John Freeman (and
Messrs. Selwyn & Blount); Mr. Norman Gale;
Mr. Edmund Gosse (and Messrs. William
Heinemann, Ltd.); Mr. Robert Graves (and
Messrs. William Heinemann, Ltd.); Mr.
Thomas Hardy (and Messrs. Macmillan & Co.)
for the epitaph, " I never cared for life," from
Late Lyrics and Earlier ; Mr. A. E. Housman
(and Mr. Grant Richards) for the " Epitaph on
an Army of Mercenaries," from *Last Poems ;*
Dr. Walter Leaf (and Mr. Grant Richards) for
four translations from *Little Poems from the
Greek ;* Mr. Shane Leslie (and Messrs. Burns
Oates & Washbourne); Miss Winifred Lucas
(and Mr. John Lane); Mr. Wilfrid Meynell
(and Messrs. Burns Oates & Washbourne);
Mr. J. B. B. Nichols; Mr. Eden Phillpotts
(with Mr. Cecil Palmer for " Nature and the
Dead Artist," from *Delight*, and with Mr. Grant
Richards for " The Fair," from *Cherry Stones*);
Miss Margaret Postgate; Mr. J. B. Priestley
(and Messrs. Bowes and Bowes) for four epi-
grams from *Brief Diversions ;* Sir A. Quiller-
Couch (and Messrs. Cassells); Mr. Frederick
Reynolds; Lady Margaret Sackville; Mr. Sieg-
fried Sassoon (and Messrs. William Heinemann,

Ltd.); Mr. J. C. Squire (and Messrs. Hodder & Stoughton); Mr. J. St. Loe Strachey; Mr. L. A. G. Strong (and Mr. B. H. Blackwell); Mr. Arthur Symons (and Messrs. William Heinemann, Ltd.); Mr. H. T. Wade-Gery (and the Golden Cockerel Press); Sir William Watson (and Mr. John Lane); Miss Anna Wickham (and Mr. Grant Richards) for four epigrams from *The Man with a Hammer*; and Mr. I. A. Williams.

I have also to thank the literary executor of the late A. H. Bullen (and Messrs. Sidgwick & Jackson, Ltd.) for an epigram; Sir Henry Newbolt for three epigrams from *Poems* (Messrs. Elkin Matthews) by Mary E. Coleridge; Mr. John Lane for two epigrams by Francis Coutts, Lord Latymer; the executors of the late Austin Dobson for his epigram "On Didactics in Poetry " (p. 67); Mr. John Lane for two epigrams by Ernest Dowson; Mr. R. S. Garnett for five epigrams by Richard Garnett from *Idylls and Epigrams*; Mrs. Welby-Everard (and Messrs. Macmillan & Co.) for an epigram by Maurice Hewlett from *Helen Redeemed*; Messrs. Elkin Matthews, Ltd. for an epitaph by Lionel Johnson; Mrs. Andrew Lang (and Messrs. Longmans Green & Co.) for three epigrams by Andrew Lang from his *Poetical Works*; Mrs. MacDonagh (and Messrs. Hodges, Figgis & Co.) for an epigram by Thomas MacDonagh; Mr. William Meredith and the Trustees to the estate of the late George Meredith (and Messrs. Constable & Co.) for an epitaph by George Meredith; Mr. Wilfrid Meynell (and Messrs. Burns Oates & Washbourne) for epigrams by Alice Meynell, by Francis Thompson and by John Banister

Tabb ; Mrs. Patmore (and Messrs. G. Bell & Sons, Ltd.) for five epigrams by Coventry Patmore ; Mr. John Lane for an epigram by Stephen Phillips ; Sir Herbert Stephen (and Messrs. Bowes & Bowes) for an epigram by J. K. Stephen ; Messrs. P. J. and A. E. Dobell for two epigrams by James Thomson (B.V.) ; Messrs. Burns Oates & Washbourne for two epigrams and an epitaph by Aubrey de Vere.

If I have overlooked any rights, I trust I may be forgiven.

Finally, I should like to acknowledge the help I have derived from several previous collections of epigrams, however much I have usually disagreed with the taste of their compilers ; in particular I am indebted to the Rev. H. P. Dodd's *The Epigrammatists* (1870), an erudite work with which, purely as a book for students, I have neither the wish nor the ability to compete.

G. R. H.

INDEX OF AUTHORS†

† For sources of anonymous epigrams, see at end
of Index.

† I have been unable to find out anything about this man. His poem appears in early XVIIIth century collections.

† The epitaph on p. 148 is not included, so far as I can find, in any edition of Shenstone. It is, however, attributed to him on the reliable authority of *The Festoon* (2nd edition, 1767), an anthology by his friend the Rev. Richard Graves.

ANONYMOUS EPIGRAMS

(The text of a particular epigram occasionally follows a later version than that of the book quoted.)

Orlando Gibbons' First Set of Madrigals, 1612 : 57.

Camden's Remains, 1623 : 12, 134, 153.

Wit's Recreations, 1640 : 5, 7, 14, 104, 105, 112, 120, 121, 134, 135 (2), 143, 146, 151 (2), 152, 153, 155.

Wit Restored, 1658 : 4.

Dr. John Wilson's Cheerful Airs or Ballads, 1660 : 80.

Poems on State Affairs, 1704 : 33.

The Spectator, No. 551, 1712 : 74.

Steele's Miscellany, 1714 : 58.

Lewis's First Miscellany, 1726 : 22, 149, 167.

A Collection of Epigrams, 1727 : 20, 26, 31, 47, 49, 74.

Jones's Curious Collection of Epitaphs, 1727 : 13, 106, 132, 142, 144, 147, 151, 152, 153, 154, 156, 158, 159, 168.

Certain Epigrams in Laud and Praise of the Gentlemen of the Dunciad (*N.D.*) : 65.

A Collection of Epigrams (2nd Edition, *Vol. II*), 1737 : 25, 33, 36.

The Daily Gazetteer, 1738 : 65.

Epigrams in Distich, 1740 : 7, 22, 26.

Birch Manuscripts in the British Museum : 3.

Toldervy's Select Epitaphs, 1755 : 145.

Hackett's Select and Remarkable Epitaphs, 1757 : 150.

The Christmas Treat (*Dublin*), 1767 : 150.

Poems selected from The Shamrock, or Hibernian Cresses (2nd Edition), 1774 : 50.

Webb's New Select Collection of Epitaphs, 1775 : 5, 20.

New Foundling Hospital for Wit, 1784 : 16.

An Asylum for Fugitive Pieces, 1785 : 36, 67.

Headley's Select Beauties of Ancient English Poetry, 1787 : 139.

Dodd's Select Epigrams, 1797 : 3, 5, 45.

Frobisher's New Select Collection of Epitaphs, c. 1800 : 148.

Poetical Register (*Vol. II*), 1803 : 72.

A Collection of Epitaphs, 1806 : 122.

Notes and Queries, 15th March, 1854 : 159.

Pettigrew's Select Collection of Epitaphs, 1857 : 141.

Norfolk's Collection of Curious Epitaphs, 1861 : 4, 12 (3), 14, 152.

Booth's Metrical Epitaphs, 1868 : 4, 26.

Dodd's Epigrammatists, 1870 : 173.

Fairley's Epitaphiana, 1875 : 9, 38.

Stewart's Epigrams and Epitaphs, 1897 : 32, 37.

Nursery Rhyme (? date) : 7.

Worcestershire Epitaph (? date) : 100.

THE
SOUL OF WIT

§ I

MAINLY HUMOROUS AND SATIRICAL

TO VULCAN

Robert Herrick

Thy sooty Godhead I desire
Still to be ready with thy fire :
That, should my book despisèd be,
Acceptance it might find of thee.

TO HIS BOOK

Samuel Sheppard

Go forth in thine own strength amid the
    crowd,
Be not thou too submiss, nor yet too proud ;
If any jostle, stand the sturdy shock,
Have I not fixt thee firmer than a rock ?

b

ON THE LATIN GERUNDS
Richard Porson

When Dido found Æneas would not come,
She mourn'd in silence, and was Di-do-dum.

A REFLECTION
Thomas Hood

When Eve upon the first of men
  The apple pressed with specious cant,
Oh ! what a thousand pities then
  That Adam was not adamant.

ON MR. JUSTICE ASHURST
Lord Erskine

Judge Ashurst, with his lantern jaws,
Throws light upon the English laws.

ON LORD KENMARE AND DANIEL O'CONNELL

HESITATING TO FIGHT A DUEL WITH SIR C. SAXTON,
THE ONE ON ACCOUNT OF HIS SICK DAUGHTER, THE
OTHER THROUGH THE INTERFERENCE OF HIS WIFE.

Thomas Moore

These heroes of Erin, abhorrent of slaughter,
  Improve on the Jewish command ;
One honours his wife, and the other his
    daughter,
  That their days may be long in the land.

ON J. W. WARD
Samuel Rogers

Ward has no heart, they say ; but I deny it ;—
He has a heart, and gets his speeches by it.

DISINHERITED
John Donne

Thy father all from thee, by his last will,
Gave to the poor ; thou hast good title still.

ON THE ABBEY CHURCH AT BATH
Henry Harington, M.D.

These walls, so full of monument and bust,
Show how Bath waters serve to lay the dust.

ON ARCHBISHOP POTTER,
Ob. 1747
From the Birch MSS. (letter of August 1747)

Alack, and well-a-day,
Potter himself is turn'd to clay !

ON FOOTE, THE COMEDIAN
From Dodd's Select Epigrams, 1797.

Foote from his earthly stage, alas ! is hurl'd ;
Death took him off, who took off all the world.

ON MR. PARTRIDGE
From Norfolk's Epitaphs, 1861.

What! kill a partridge in the month of May!
Was that done like a sportsman? Eh,
    Death, eh?

ON JOHN GRUBB
From Booth's Epitaphs, 1868.

When from the chrysalis of the tomb
I rise in rainbow-colour'd plume,
My weeping friends, ye scarce will know
That I was but a Grubb below.

ON BOND THE USURER
From Wit Restored, 1658.

Here lies a Bond under this tomb
Seal'd and deliver'd to God knows whom.

IN OBITUM PROMI
Henry Parrot

That Death should thus from hence our
    Butler catch,
Into my mind it cannot quickly sink;
Sure Death came thirsty to the Buttery
    Hatch
When he (that busy was) denied him drink.
Tut, 'twas not so: 'tis like he gave him
    liquor,
And Death, made drunk, took him away the
    quicker—
    Yet let not others grieve too much in mind,
    (The Butler gone) the keys are left behind.

IN RICHARDUM
Thomas Freeman

At three go-downs Dick doffs me off a pot :
The English gutter's Latin for his throat.

ON MR. JOSEPH SHARPE,
NEEDLEMAKER
AND COMMON-COUNCILMAN OF FARRINGDON WITHOUT
From Webb's Epitaphs, 1775

Alas ! he's dead, good Master Sharpe !
Could I, like David, thrum the Harp,
I would his Virtues here rehearse,
In humble Common Council Verse.
But who can Butcher Death, pray, wheedle ?
He from his Hand snatch'd out a Needle ;
A Needle sharper than his Dart,
And stuck it into Joseph's Heart.

ON MR. STONE
From Wit's Recreations, 1640.

Jerusalem's curse is not fulfill'd in me,
For here a stone upon a stone you see.

ON THE PHRASE, "TO KILL TIME"
From Voltaire: Dodd's Select Epigrams, 1797

There's scarce a point whereon mankind
    agree
So well, as in their boast of killing me :
I boast of nothing, but, when I've a mind,
I think I can be even with mankind.

THE GRAND TOUR

Samuel Boyce

Quoth his heir to Sir John,
  " I'd to travel begone,
Like others, the world for to see."
  Quoth Sir John to his heir,
  " Prithee, novice, forbear,
For I'd not have the world to see thee."

AT NEWMARKET

Samuel Bishop

See on Newmarket's turf, my lord
  Instructs his jockey how to trim ;
Who, to make sure of full reward,
  First cheats all round—and then cheats
    him.
What similar parts extremes assume !
Like groom, like peer ! like peer, like groom !

OF A FALLING METEOR

John Donne, the younger

An astrologian in a moonshine night
Taking the altitude of a star's height
With 's Jacob's staff erected towards the sky,
It chanc'd a meteor fell down instantly ;
At which a country clown a great shout
    making,
His Jacob's staff then for a crossbow taking,
Thinking he'd hit a star, unto him saith,
" Thou'rt a brave marksman, O well shot
    i' faith ! "

Sing a song,
When Adam delved

IN GETAM
Thomas Bastard

Geta from wool and weaving first began,
Swelling and swelling to a Gentleman ;
When he was Gentleman and bravely dight,
He left not swelling till he was a knight :
At last (forgetting what he was at first)
He swole to be a Lord, and then he burst.

HISTORY
A Nursery Rhyme

Bluff Harry the Eighth to six spouses was
    wedded :
One died, one survived, two divorced, two
    beheaded.

ON EVE'S APPLES
From Wit's Recreations, 1640

Eve, for thy fruit thou gav'st too dear a price.
What ? for an apple give a Paradise ?
If nowadays of fruit such gains were made,
A costermonger were a devilish trade.

ON A PROUD FELLOW
From Epigrams in Distich, 1740

Jack his own merit sees : this gives him
    pride,
That he sees more than all the world beside.

ON BIBULUS
Robert Heath

Here, who but once in 's life did thirst, doth
    lie ;
Perhaps the dust may make him once more
    dry.

ON THRASO
William Walsh

Thraso picks quarrels when he's drunk at
    night ;
When sober in the morning dares not fight.
Thraso, to shun those ills that may ensue,
Drink not at night, or drink at morning too.

THE HEIR
Leonard Welsted

I owe, says Metius, much to Colon's care ;
Once only seen, he chose me for his heir :
True, Metius ; hence your fortunes take
    their rise ;
His heir you were not, had he seen you twice.

ON HEARING THAT THERE WAS FALSEHOOD IN THE REV. DR. BABINGTON'S VERY LOOKS
Robert Burns

That there is falsehood in his looks
    I must and will deny ;
They say their master is a knave—
    And sure they do not lie.

EPITAPH BY A SON
From Fairley's Epitaphiana, 1875

Beneath this stone, in hopes of Zion,
Doth lie the landlord of the Lion ;
His son keeps on the business still,
Resigned unto the heavenly will.

ON JOHN ADAMS, OF SOUTHWELL
Lord Byron

John Adams lies here, of the parish of
    Southwell,
A Carrier who carried his can to his mouth
    well :
He carried so much, and he carried so fast,
He could carry no more—so was carried at
    last ;
For, the liquor he drank, being too much for
    one,
He could not carry off,—so he's now carri-on.

ON THE WORDS "DOMUS ULTIMA"
INSCRIBED ON THE VAULT BELONGING TO THE DUKES OF
RICHMOND
William Clarke

Did he, who thus inscrib'd the wall,
Not read, or not believe S. Paul,
Who says there is, where'er it stands,
Another house not made with hands ;
Or may we gather from these words,
That house is not a house of Lords ?

A SERIOUS DANGER
R. A. Davenport

Sylla declares the world shall know
That he's my most determined foe !
I wish him wide the tale to spread ;
For all that I from Sylla dread
Is, that the knave, to serve some end,
May one day swear that he's my friend.

OF TREASON
Sir John Harington

Treason doth never prosper ; what's the
    reason ?
For if it prosper, none dare call it treason.

FROM THE FRENCH OF M. FRANCIS MAYNARD*
Charles Cotton

Anthony feigns him sick of late,
    Only to show how he at home
Lies in a princely Bed of State,
    And in a nobly furnish'd Room,
        Adorn'd with Pictures of Vandike's,
        A pair of Crystal Candlesticks,
            Rich Carpets, Quilts, the Devil, and
                all :
        Then you, his careful friends, if ever
        You wish to cure him of his fever,
            Go lodge him in the Hospital.

* The French in its turn appears to be an imitation
of Martial (Book II, 16).

IN ROMAM
Sir John Harington

Hate and debate Rome through the world
    hath spread,
Yet *Roma Amor* is, if backward read.
    Then is't not strange Rome hate should
        foster ? No :
    For out of backward love, all hate doth
        grow.

ON COBB AND WEBB, A FIRM IN WESTMINSTER
J. C. Squire

So fit and final a conjunction here,
    The mint of human wit could never coin,
Eternal Purpose did not show more clear
    Through Plato's halves predestinate to
        join.

ON MR. BUTLER'S MONUMENT
Samuel Wesley

Whilst Butler, needy wretch ! was yet alive,
No gen'rous patron would a dinner give :
See him, when starved to death, and turn'd
    to dust,
Presented with a monumental bust !
The poet's fate is here in emblem shown,—
He ask'd for bread, and he receiv'd a stone.

AT LEEDS

From Norfolk's Epitaphs, 1861

Here lies my wife,
Here lies she ;
Hallelujah !
Hallelujee !

CHELTENHAM WATERS

From Norfolk's Epitaphs, 1861

Here lie I and my four daughters,
Killed by drinking Cheltenham waters.
Had we but stuck to Epsom salts,
We wouldn't have been in these here vaults.

UPON A LOCKSMITH

From Camden's Remains, 1623

A zealous locksmith died of late,
And did arrive at Heaven's gate.
He stood without, and would not knock,
Because he meant to pick the lock.

AT EDINBURGH

From Norfolk's Epitaphs, 1861

Here lie I, Martin Eldinbrode,
Ha' mercy on my soul, Lord Gode,
As I would do, were I Lord Gode,
And thou wert Martin Eldinbrode.

ON ONE NAM'D JOHN

(It was his usual custom in company, when he told them anything, to ask, *D'ye hear?* And if any said, he did not hear him, John would reply, *No matter, I've said*).

From A Curious Collection of Epitaphs, 1727

Death came to John,
    And whisper'd in his ear,
You must die, John ;
        D'ye hear ?

Quoth John to Death,
    The news is bad :
No matter, quoth Death,
        I've said.

ON PETER STAGGS
John Wolcot

Poor Peter Staggs now rests beneath this rail,
Who loved his joke, his pipe, and mug of
    ale ;
For twenty years he did the duties well,
Of ostler, boots, and waiter, at the " Bell " :
But Death stepp'd in, and ordered Peter
    Staggs
To feed his worms and leave the farmer's
    nags.
The clock struck one, alas ! 'twas Peter's
    knell,
Who sigh'd, " I'm coming—that's the
    ostler's bell."

JOHNNY DOW
From Norfolk's Epitaphs, 1861

Wha lies here ?
I, Johnny Dow.
Hoo ! Johnny, is that you ?
Ay, man, but a'm dead now.

ON A PORTER
From Wit's Recreations, 1640

At length by works of wondrous Fate,
Here lies the Porter of Winchester-Gate :
If gone to Heav'n, as much I fear,
He can but be a Porter there :
He fear'd not Hell so much for 's sin,
As for th' great rapping, and oft coming-in.

UPON PARSON BEANES
Robert Herrick

Old Parson Beanes hunts six days of the
    week,
And on the seventh, he has his notes to seek.
Six days he hollows so much breath away,
That on the seventh he can nor preach nor
    pray.

TO ALCHEMISTS
Ben Jonson

If all you boast of your great art be true ;
Sure, willing poverty lives most in you.

ON A FAT DOCTOR

Abel Evans

When Tadlow walks the streets, the paviours
    cry,
"God bless you, sir!" and lay their ram-
    mers by.

ON THE BURSAR OF ST. JOHN'S COLLEGE, OXON, CUTTING DOWN A FINE ROW OF TREES

Dr. Tadlow or Dr. Conyers*

Indulgent Nature on each kind bestows
A secret instinct to discern its foes :
The goose, a silly bird, avoids the fox ;
Lambs fly from wolves ; and sailors steer
    from rocks ;
A rogue the gallows, as his fate, foresees,
And bears the like antipathy to trees.

ON *Who wrote Icon Basilike?* BY DR. CHRISTOPHER WORDSWORTH, MASTER OF TRINITY

Benjamin Hall Kennedy

Who wrote *Who wrote Icon Basilike?*
I, said the Master of Trinity,
With my small ability,
I wrote *Who wrote Icon Basilike?*

---

* Dr. Tadlow, I hope, the Bursar being Abel Evans.

EPITAPH ON COLBERT, MINISTER OF LOUIS XIV

FROM THE FRENCH

R. A. Davenport

Here lies the father of taxation :
   May Heaven, his faults forgiving,
   Grant him repose ; which he, while
     living,
Would never grant the nation.

ON RAISING THE LAND TAX FOR 1776

From the New Foundling Hospital for Wit,
1784

Four shillings in the pound we see,
   And well may be contented,
Since wars, that ne'er were meant to be,
   Are happily prevented.

Besides, North absolute become,
   Might plunder every penny ;
Then blame him not for taking some,
   Thank him for leaving any.

JOHN BULL

Lord Byron

The world is a bundle of hay,
   Mankind are the asses who pull ;
Each tugs it a different way,
   And the greatest of all is John Bull.

THE INFERENCE
Philip Dodd

Joe hates a sycophant. It shows
Self-love is not a fault of Joe's.

THE SAME COMPLAINT
Norman Gale

" What's your most vexing parasite,"
    Bawled Earth to Mars, " since Life
        began ? "
Mars roared an answer through the night,
    In emphasis of thunder, " Man ! "

UPON A COMPANY OF BAD DANCERS TO GOOD MUSIC
George Jeffreys

How ill the motion to the music suits !
So Orpheus fiddled, and so danced the
    brutes.

ON ADMIRAL VERNON'S APPOINTMENT TO PRESIDE OVER THE HERRING FISHERY
Horace Walpole

Long in the senate had brave Vernon rail'd,
And all mankind with bitter tongue assail'd ;
Sick of his noise, we wearied Heav'n with
    pray'r,
In his own element to place the tar.
The gods at length have yielded to our wish,
And bade him rule o'er Billingsgate and fish.

c

ON A LADY PLAYING PATIENCE
J. C. Squire

" I shall play Patience," Delia said,
" To soothe me till I go to bed."
She failed, and failed, and failed once more,
Then flung the cards upon the floor.

HONESTY AT A FIRE
J. C. Squire

What a calamity ! What dreadful loss !
 How sad 'twould be if anyone were dead.
Still no fire engine ! Look, it leaps across !
 O how I hope this lovely fire will spread !

ON A LORD
Samuel Taylor Coleridge

Here lies the Devil—ask no other name.
Well—but you mean Lord ——? Hush ! we
 mean the same.

ON SIR WALTER SCOTT'S POEM "THE FIELD OF WATERLOO"
Lord Erskine

On Waterloo's ensanguined plain
Lie tens of thousands of the slain ;
But none, by sabre or by shot,
Fell half as flat as Walter Scott.

QUIT
Matthew Prior

To John I ow'd great obligation ;
  But John unhappily thought fit
To publish it to all the nation :
  Sure John and I are more than quit.

ON A SCHOOLMASTER IN CLEISH PARISH, KINROSS-SHIRE
Robert Burns

Here lie Willie Michie's banes ;
  O Satan, when ye tak him,
Gie him the schoolin' o' your weans,
  For clever deils he'll mak' em !

AN IMPROMPTU IN A KIRK GALLERY, EDINBURGH
A. Davidson Parker

Oh ! Roger, tak' y'r rod and creel
And haud y'r clatter o' the Deil ;
Though ye may catch the troot and podly,
Ye'll never mak' the sinner godly.

Though by y'r claith ye are nae doot
A fisher mair o' men than troot,
Yet, gin ye cast y'r line that gait
Nae human fish will tak' y'r bait.

RICHARD HIND
From Webb's Epitaphs, 1775
Here lies the body of Richard Hind,
Who was neither ingenious, sober, nor kind.

THE MISTAKEN RESOLVE
*After Martial : from A Collection of
Epigrams*, 1727
Thou swear'st thou'lt drink no more ; kind
     heaven send
Me such a cook or coachman, but no friend.

THE FIVE REASONS FOR DRINKING
Henry Aldrich
If all be true that I do think,
There are five reasons we should drink ;
Good wine—a friend—or being dry—
Or lest we should be by and by—
Or any other reason why.

ON A CERTAIN LORD'S GIVING
SOME THOUSAND POUNDS FOR A
HOUSE
David Garrick
So many thousands for a house
For you, of all the world, Lord Mouse !
A little house would best accord
With you, my very little lord !
And then exactly match'd would be
Your house and hospitality.

ON WATER-DRINKERS

Philip Smyth : from Antipater of Sidon

Not Pleiads, dreadful to the Western Main,
The angry seas, which dash on yon proud
    rock,
Nor the loud thunder rolling o'er the plain,
With equal horrors can my bosom shock,
As the pale water-drinker, who to light
Ushers the mad'ning follies of the night.

ADVICE

Richard Garnett : from Marcus Argentarius

Thou art in danger, Cincius, on my word,
To die ere thou hast lived, which were
    absurd.
Open thine ears to song, thy throat to wine,
Thy arms unto that pretty wife of thine.
Philosophy, I have nowise forgot,
Is deathless, but philosophers are not.

IN CHAUCER'S STYLE

Matthew Prior

Full oft doth Mat. with Topaz dine,
Eateth baked meats, drinketh Greek wine ;
But Topaz his own werke rehearseth,
And Mat. mote praise what Topaz verseth.
Now sure as priest did e'er shrive sinner,
Full hardly earneth Mat. his dinner.

VERSES WROTE AT BRIGADIER
S——'
OVER A BOWL OF PUNCH, WHERE JUPITER AND HEBE
WERE PAINTED IN THE CEILING
From Lewis's First Miscellany, 1726

Let Jove no more his Hebe boast,
    Or quaff celestial wine ;
We here have many a brighter toast,
    And nectar more divine.

What place more fram'd for mirth and love
    Could Art or Nature show ?
The merry Thund'rer rules above,
    The Brigadier below.

A MISER'S INVITATION
From Epigrams in Distich, 1740

His chimneys smoke ! it is some omen dire !
His neighbours are alarm'd ; and cry out,
    Fire !

CLAY
Richard Garnett

Both thou and I alike, my Bacchic urn,
From clay are sprung, and must to clay
    return ;
But happier fate this day is mine and thine,
For I am full of life, and thou of wine ;
Our powers for mutual aid united be,
Keep thou me blithe, and flowing I'll keep
    thee.

ON A BROKEN PIPE
James Thomson (B.V.)

Neglected now it lies, a cold clay form,
So late with living inspirations warm :
Type of all other creatures formed of clay—
What more than it for Epitaph have they ?

OCCASIONED BY A SERMON FOR THE CHARITY CHILDREN AT TUNBRIDGE WELLS
Mary Barber

So little giv'n at chapel door !—
This people, doubtless, must be poor !
So much at gaming thrown away !—
No nation sure, so rich as they !

Britons, 'twere greatly for your glory,
Should those, who shall transmit your story,
Their notion of your grandeur frame,
Not as you give, but as you game.

ON MRS. TOFTS, A CELEBRATED SINGER
Alexander Pope

So bright is thy beauty, so charming thy song,
As had drawn both the beasts and their
    Orpheus along ;
But such is thy avarice, and such is thy
    pride,
That the beasts must have starv'd, and the
    poet have dy'd.

HERMANN
Richard Porson

The Germans in Greek
Are sadly to seek ;
Not five in five score,
But ninety-five more,—
All, save only Hermann,
    And Hermann's a German.

WRITTEN OVER A GATE
Duke of Buckinghamshire

Here lives a man, who, by relation,
Depends upon predestination ;
For which the learned and the wise
His understanding much despise :
But I pronounce with loyal tongue
Him in the right, them in the wrong ;
For how could such a wretch succeed
But that, alas, it was *decreed?*

A VILLAGE CONFLICT
Robert Graves

The cottage damson laden as could be
Scowls at the Manor House magnolia tree
That year by year within its thoughtless
    powers
Yields flowers and leaves and flowers and
    leaves and flowers,
While the magnolia shudders as in fear,
" *Figurez-vous !* two sackfuls every year ! "

ON THE BUSTS IN RICHMOND
HERMITAGE, 1732
Jonathan Swift

Lewis the living genius fed,
And rais'd the scientific head ;
Our Queen, more frugal of her meat,
Raises those heads that cannot eat.

THE ABOVE, ANSWERED
From A Collection of Epigrams, 1737

Our Queen, more anxious to be just
Than flatter'd, rears the living bust
To chosen spirits, learned tribe !
Whom, Lewis like, she cannot bribe.

INVENTIONS
Samuel Butler

All the inventions that the world contains,
Were not by reason first found out, nor
      brains ;
But pass for theirs who had the luck to light
Upon them by mistake or oversight.

TO DOCTOR EMPIRIC
Ben Jonson

When men a dangerous disease did 'scape,
Of old, they gave a cock to Æsculape ;
Let me give two, that doubly am got free ;
From my disease's danger, and from thee.

ON A SHARPER
From Epigrams in Distich, 1740

Townly accuses Fortune, every day ;
So will not I, when I with Townly play.

ON A SHARK
I. A. Williams

C.'s jolly countenance is free from guile—
Which knows its place, and keeps behind his
    smile.

ON DR. CADE'S DYING BY HIS OWN RECIPE
From A Collection of Epigrams, 1727

Cade, who had slain ten thousand men
With that small instrument, a pen,
Being sick, unluckily he try'd
The point upon himself, and dy'd.

ON ONE WHO DIED WHILE HIS PHYSICIAN WAS WRITING A PRESCRIPTION FOR HIM
From Booth's Epitaphs, 1868

How couldst thou thus so hasty be, O
    Death ?
And why be so precipitate with me ?
Why not some moments longer spare my
    breath,
    And let thy friend, the doctor, get his fee ?

TWO PHYSICIANS
Joseph Jekyll

See one physician, like a sculler, plies,
The patient lingers and by inches dies.
But two physicians, like a pair of oars,
Waft him more swiftly to the Stygian shores.

DEMOPHILUS
Henry Wellesley : from Nicarchus

The screech-owl sings ; death follows at her
cries :
Demophilus strikes up ; the screech-owl
dies.

ON PETER ROBINSON
Francis Jeffrey, Lord Jeffrey (?)

Here lies the preacher, judge and poet,
Peter,
Who broke the laws of God, and man, and
metre.

VANITY
James Thomson (B.V.)

Once in a saintly passion
    I cried with desperate grief,
O Lord, my heart is black with guile,
    Of sinners I am chief.
Then stooped my guardian angel
    And whispered from behind,
" Vanity, my little man,
    You're nothing of the kind."

THE VINE AND THE GOAT

A. C. Benson : from Evenus

What though thou crop my branches to the
　　root,
Yet will I bear one cluster more of fruit ;—
One cluster more, that shall for wine suffice
To make libation at thy sacrifice.

THE BETTER WAY

Walter Leaf : from Nicarchus

If you desire to paralyse
Your enemy, don't " d——n his eyes " ;
From futile blasphemy desist ;
Send him to —— the oculist.

ON DEMAR, THE USURER

Ob. 6th July 1720

Jonathan Swift

Beneath this verdant hillock lies
Demar, the wealthy and the wise.
His heirs, that he might safely rest,
Have put his carcase in a chest :
The very chest in which, they say,
His other self, his money, lay.
And if his heirs continue kind
To that dear self he left behind,
I dare believe that four in five
Will think his better self alive.

ENGRAVED ON THE COLLAR OF A DOG, WHICH I GAVE TO HIS ROYAL HIGHNESS

Alexander Pope

I am his Highness' dog at Kew ;
Pray tell me, sir, whose dog are you ?

TIME

W. S. Landor

The burden of an ancient rhyme
Is " By the forelock seize on Time."
Time in some corner heard it said ;
Pricking his ears, away he fled ;
And, seeing me upon the road,
A hearty curse on me bestow'd.
" What if I do the same by thee ?
How wouldst thou like it ? " thunder'd he ;
And, without answer thereupon,
Seizing *my* forelock . . . it was gone.

CLOE'S PERJURY

Thomas Freeman

'Tis one of Cloe's qualities,
That ever when she swears she lies :
Dost love me, Cloe ? swear not so,
For when thou swear'st, thou liest I know :
Dost hate me, Cloe ? prythee swear,
For then I know thou lov'st me dear.

ON SIR JOHN VANBRUGH,
ARCHITECT
Abel Evans

Under this stone, reader, survey
Dead Sir John Vanbrugh's house of clay.
Lie heavy on him, earth ! for he
Laid many heavy loads on thee.

THE POWER OF TIME
Jonathan Swift

If neither brass nor marble can withstand
The mortal force of Time's destructive hand ;
If mountains sink to vales, if cities die,
And lessening rivers mourn their fountains
    dry ;
When my old cassock (said a Welsh divine)
Is out at elbows, why should I repine ?

AN ARGUMENT
TO ANY PHILLIS OR CHLOE
Thomas Moore

I've oft been told by learned friars
    That wishing and the crime are one,
And Heaven punishes desires
    As much as if the deed were done.

If wishing damns us, you and I
    Are damn'd to all our heart's content ;
Come, then, at least we may enjoy
    Some pleasure for our punishment.

LINGUA POTENTIOR ARMIS

From A Collection of Epigrams, 1727

That speech surpasses force, is no new whim :
Jove caus'd the heav'ns to tremble ; Juno
    him.

ON A COUNTRY LAIRD

Robert Burns

Bless Jesus Christ, O Cardoness,
    With grateful lifted eyes,
Who said that not the soul alone,
    But body too, must rise ;
For had he said " The soul alone
    From death I will deliver,"
Alas ! alas ! O Cardoness,
    Then hadst thou lain for ever !

A REASONABLE AFFLICTION

Matthew Prior

On his death-bed poor Lubin lies ;
    His spouse is in despair :
With frequent sobs, and mutual cries,
    They both express their care.

" A different cause," says parson Sly,
    " The same effect may give :
Poor Lubin fears that he shall die ;
    His wife, that he may live."

ON ALDERMAN W——
THE HISTORY OF HIS LIFE

John Cunningham

That he was born it cannot be denied,
He ate, drank, slept, talk'd politics, and died.

ON THOMAS, SECOND EARL OF ONSLOW

From Stewart's Epigrams and Epitaphs, 1897

What can Tommy Onslow do ?
Drive a phaeton and two.
Can Tommy Onslow do no more ?
Yes ; drive a phaeton and four.

ON AN INSIGNIFICANT FELLOW
FROM THE FRENCH

Lord Curzon of Kedleston

Colley fell ill, and is no more !
His fate you bid me to deplore ;
But what the deuce is to be said ?
Colley was living, Colley's dead.

ON A CERTAIN WILL

I. A. Williams

A., of fish a mighty taker,
Knows 'tis time to face his Maker ;
Yet, ere he steps before his God,
Halts to bequeath his fishing-rod.

ON PUGLEY, A DON
Hilaire Belloc

Pugley denies the Soul : why, so do I
The soul of Pugley heartily deny.

ON PETER ARETIN
From A Collection of Epigrams, 1737

Here Aretin interr'd doth lie,
  Whose satire lash'd both high and low :
His God alone it spar'd ; and why ?
  His God, he said, he did not know.

ELEGY ON COLEMAN
From Poems on State Affairs, 1704

If heav'n be pleas'd when sinners cease to
    sin,
If hell be pleas'd when souls are damn'd
    therein,
If earth be pleas'd when it's rid of a knave,
Then all are pleas'd, for Coleman's in his
    grave.

ON THE DEATH OF X
*F. P. Barnard : paraphrase of Eurichius
Cordus*

When X deceased and passed below,
Earth jumped for joy. " For you 'tis well,"
Said Nick, " but I should like to know
Why was this monster sent to Hell ? "

                                    d

OF COMMON DEVOTION
Francis Quarles

Our God and soldiers we alike adore
Ev'n at the brink of danger ; not before :
After deliverance, both alike requited,
Our God's forgotten, and our soldiers
    slighted.

THE BALANCE OF EUROPE
Alexander Pope

Now Europe's balanc'd, neither side pre-
    vails,
For nothing's left in either of the scales.

TO THE FRENCH KING
OCCASIONED BY THE BATTLE
OF DETTINGEN
Thomas Newcomb

The fates of Bourbon laurels yield,
    Nor George's rival sword forget ;
George always conquers in the field,
    Bourbon as oft in the Gazette.

What monarch's fame would shine so bright,
    So fair a lustre round diffuse,
Were Lewis victor in the fight,
    Oft as he conquers in the news ?

INTENDED TO ALLAY THE VIOLENCE OF PARTY SPIRIT

John Byrom

God bless the King! I mean the Faith's
    Defender;
God bless—no harm in blessing—the Pre-
    tender!
But who Pretender is, or who is King,
God bless us all!—that's quite another thing.

THE DILEMMA

J. C. Squire

God heard the embattled nations sing and
    shout
  "Gott strafe England!" and "God save
    the King!"
God this, God that, and God the other
    thing—
"Good God!" said God, "I've got my
    work cut out."

A FOREIGN RULER

W. S. Landor

He says, *My reign is peace*, so slays
    A thousand in the dead of night.
Are you all happy now? he says,
    And those he leaves behind cry *quite*.
He swears he will have no contention,
    And sets all nations by the ears;
He shouts aloud, *No intervention!*
    Invades, and drowns them all in tears.

REVENGE

Lord Nugent

Lie on ! while my revenge shall be,
To speak the very truth of thee.

ON DR. PRETTYMAN

From An Asylum for Fugitive Pieces, 1785

Fib on, O Prettyman !—for pay :—
And thou, O Pitt, fib too !
More against Truth you cannot say,
Than Truth has said 'gainst you.

ON DR. B—NTL—Y'S APPLYING TO HIMSELF THESE LINES:

*—Sunt et mihi carmina ; me quoque dicunt
Vatem pastores : sed non ego credulus illis.*

From A Collection of Epigrams, 1737

How could vile sycophants contrive
A lie so great to raise ?
Which even B——y can't believe,
Tho' spoke in his own praise.

OF BOTCHING

John Heywood

God is no botcher, but when God wrought
you two,
God wrought as like a botcher, as God
might do.

A GREEK IDEA EXPANDED
From Stewart's Epigrams and Epitaphs, 1897
Of Graces four, of Muses ten,
  Of Venuses now two are seen ;
Doris shines forth to dazzle men,
  A Grace, a Muse, and Beauty's Queen ;
But let me whisper one thing more :—
The Furies now are likewise four.

DEGREES
Sir Walter Raleigh : from Pausanias
One fire than other burns more forcibly ;
  One wolf than other wolves does bite
    more sore ;
One hawk than other hawks more swift doth
    fly ;
  So one most mischievous of men before,
Callicrates, false knave as knave might be,
  Met with Menalcidas, more false than he.

SELF-KNOWLEDGE
Lord Nugent
We thought you without titles great,
And wealthy with a small estate ;
While by your humble self alone
You seem'd unrated and unknown.
But now on fortune's swelling tide
High-borne, in all the pomp of pride,
Of grandeur vain, and fond of pelf—
'Tis plain, my Lord, you knew yourself.

CHLOE
Lord Lansdowne

Bright as the day, and like the morning fair,
Such Chloe is—and common as the air.

ON LADY POLTAGRUE, A PUBLIC PERIL
Hilaire Belloc

The Devil, having nothing else to do,
Went off to tempt My Lady Poltagrue.
My Lady, tempted by a private whim,
To his extreme annoyance, tempted him.

ON A POLITICIAN
Hilaire Belloc

Here richly, with ridiculous display,
The Politician's corpse was laid away.
While all of his acquaintance sneered and
    slanged,
I wept : for I had longed to see him hanged.

A FOOL'S EPITAPH
From Fairley's Epitaphiana, 1875

Stop, reader ! I have left a world
    In which there was a world to do ;
Fretting and stewing to be rich—
    Just such a fool as you.

ON LORD GALLOWAY

Robert Burns

Bright ran thy line, O Galloway,
　　Thro' many a far-fam'd sire ;
So ran the far-fam'd Roman way,
　　So ended in a mire !

THE CRIMEAN HEROES

W. S. Landor

Hail, ye indomitable heroes, hail !
Despite of all your generals ye prevail.

THE GENERAL

Siegfried Sassoon

" Good morning ; good morning ! " the
　　General said
When we met him last week on our way to
　　the line.
Now the soldiers he smiled at are most of
　　'em dead,
And we're cursing his staff for incompetent
　　swine.
" He's a cheery old card," grunted Harry to
　　Jack
As they slogged up to Arras with rifle and
　　pack.
　　　　*　　　*　　　*　　　*
But he did for them both by his plan of
　　attack.

A RIDDLE SOLVED
Coventry Patmore

Kind souls, you wonder why, love you,
　　When you, you wonder why, love none.
We love, Fool, for the good we do,
　　Not that which unto us is done !

CROMEK SPEAKS
William Blake

I always take my judgment from a fool
Because his judgment is so very cool ;
Not prejudiced by feelings great or small,
Amiable state ! he cannot feel at all.

THE OATH
W. S. Landor

God's laws declare
Thou shalt not swear
By aught in heaven above or earth below.
　　Upon my honour ! Melville cries ;
　　He swears, and lies ;
Does Melville then break God's command-
　　ment ? No.

ON AN ELECTION
J. C. Squire

The battle's set 'twixt Envy, Greed and Pride.
Come, Conscience, do your Duty : choose
　　your side.

THE MONUMENT
POST FUNERA VIRTUS

Samuel Wesley

A Monster, in a course of vice grown old,
Leaves to his gaping heir his ill-gain'd gold;
Straight breathes his bust, straight are his
    virtues shown,
Their date commencing with the sculptur'd
    stone.
If on his specious marble we rely,
Pity a worth like his should ever die !
If credit to his real Life we give,
Pity a wretch like him should ever live !

A HISTORY OF PEACE

(Solitudinem faciunt, pacem appellant)

Robert Graves

Here rest in peace the bones of Henry Reece,
Dead through his bitter championship of
    Peace
Against all eagle-nosed and cynic lords
Who keep the *Pax Romana* with their swords.

Henry was only son of Thomas Reece,
Banker and sometime Justice of the Peace,
And of Jane Reece whom Thomas kept in
    dread
By *Pax Romana* of his board and bed.

ISAAC MEEK

Walter de la Mare

Hook-nosed was I ; loose-lipped. Greed
  fixed its gaze
In my young eyes ere they knew brass from
  gold.
Doomed to the blazing market-place my
  days,
A sweating chafferer of the bought, and sold.
Frowned on, and spat at, flattered and
  decried,
One only thing man asked of me—my price.
I lived, detested ; and forsaken, died,
Scorned by the Virtuous and the jest of Vice.
And now behold, you Christians, my true
  worth !
Step close : I have inherited the Earth.

DE MORTUO

William Drummond

The bawd of justice, he who laws controll'd
And made them fawn and frown as he got
  gold,
That Proteus of our state, whose heart and
  mouth
Were farther distant than is north from
  south,

That cormorant who made himself so gross
On people's ruin, and the prince's loss,
Is gone to hell ; and though he here did
    evil,
He there perchance may prove an honest
    devil.

WINDSOR POETICS

(Lines composed on the occasion of His Royal Highness the Prince Regent being seen standing between
the coffins of Henry VIII and Charles I in the royal
vault at Windsor.)

Lord Byron

Famed for contemptuous breach of sacred
    ties,
By headless Charles see heartless Henry lies :
Between them stands another sceptred
    thing—
It moves, it reigns—in all but name, a King :
Charles to his people, Henry to his wife,
In him the double tyrant starts to life :
Justice and death have mixed their dust in
    vain,
Each royal vampire wakes to life again.
Ah, what can tombs avail ! since these dis-
    gorge
The blood and dust of both—to mould a
    George.

§ II

MAINLY GALLANT

NO SORROW PECULIAR TO THE SUFFERER

William Cowper : from the Latin of Vincent Bourne

The lover, in melodious verses,
His singular distress rehearses,
Still closing with a rueful cry,
" Was ever such a wretch as I ? "
Yes ! thousands have endured before
All thy distress ; some, haply, more.
Unnumber'd Corydons complain,
And Strephons, of the like disdain ;
And if thy Chloe be of steel,
Too deaf to hear, too hard to feel ;
Not her alone that censure fits,
Nor thou alone hast lost thy wits.

THE RIVAL
F. P. Barnard : from L'Abbé de Saint Pavin
Each morn her glass a face reveals
In Chloe's eyes so fair,
That, save for it, no love she feels
And drives me to despair.
A suitor's cause can thrive but ill,
Whose Mistress is his Rival still.

ON HEARING A YOUNG LADY TOO FREQUENTLY EXCLAIM "THE DEVIL!"
From Dodd's Select Epigrams, 1797
See round her lips the ready Devils fly,
Mix with her words, and bask beneath her eye !
Pleas'd that so sweet a station should be giv'n,
They half forget they ever fell from Heav'n.

SYLVIA AND THE DEAN
Robert Dodsley
Cries Sylvia to a reverend Dean,
What reason can be given,
Since marriage is a holy thing,
That there is none in heaven ?

There are no women, he replied.
She quick returns the jest :—
Women there are, but I'm afraid
They cannot find a priest.

IN CLARINDA'S PRAYER-BOOK
Lord Lansdowne

In vain, Clarinda, night and day
For mercy to the Gods you pray :
What arrogance on heaven to call
For that which you deny to all !

ON A WASP SETTLING ON DELIA'S ARM
John Whaley

How sweetly careless Delia seems,
  (Her innocence can fear no harm)
While round th' envenom'd insect skims,
  Then settles on her snowy arm !

Ye flutt'ring beaux, and spiteful bards,
  To you this moral truth I sing :—
Sense, join'd to virtue, disregards
  Both Folly's buzz and Satire's sting.

ON ROSALINDA
William Popple

To Rosalinda's eyes, who not submit,
Fall the proud victims of her conquering
    wit ;
And all, whose dullness dares her wit despise,
Bow to the piercing influence of her eyes.
Thou then, who wishest not her slave to be,
Become but blind and deaf—and thou art
    free.

TO A PAINTER, DRAWING A LADY'S PICTURE

From A Collection of Epigrams, 1727

He who great Jove's artill'ry ap'd so well,
By real thunder and true lightning fell :
How then durst thou, with equal danger, try
To counterfeit the lightning of her eye ?
Painter, desist ; or soon th' event will prove,
That Love's as jealous of his arms as Jove.

FROM THE FRENCH

John Hughes

I die with too transporting joy,
    If she I love rewards my fire ;
If she's inexorably coy,
    With too much passion I expire.

No way the fates afford to shun
    The cruel torment I endure ;
Since I am doom'd to be undone
    By the disease or by the cure.

LOVE INCURABLE

Abraham Cowley

Sol Daphne sees, and seeing her admires,
Which adds new flames to his celestial fires :
Had any remedy for love been known,
The god of physic, sure, had cur'd his own.

THE MAIDEN'S CHOICE
Samuel Bishop

A fool and knave with different views,
    For Julia's hand apply :
The knave, to mend his fortune, sues,
    The fool, to please his eye.

Ask you, how Julia will behave ?
    Depend on't for a rule,
If she's a fool, she'll wed the knave—
    If she's a knave, the fool.

ON MISTRESS BIDDY FLOYD; OR, THE RECEIPT TO FORM A BEAUTY
Jonathan Swift

When Cupid did his grandsire Jove intreat
To form some Beauty by a new receipt,
Jove sent and found, far in a country scene,
Truth, innocence, good-nature, look serene :
From which ingredients first the dext'rous
        boy
Pick'd the demure, the awkward, and the coy ;
The Graces from the Court did next provide
Breeding, and wit, and air, and decent
        pride ;
These Venus cleans'd from every spurious
        grain
Of nice, coquet, affected, pert, and vain :
Jove mixt up all, and his best clay imploy'd ;
Then call'd the happy composition, Floyd.

TO A SEMPSTRESS

From A Collection of Epigrams, 1727

Oh what bosom but must yield,
   When, like Pallas, you advance,
With a thimble for your shield,
   And a needle for your lance ?

Fairest of the stitching train,
   Ease my passion by your art ;
And, in pity to my pain,
   Mend the hole that's in my heart.

VENUS MISTAKEN

Matthew Prior : after Leonidas of Tarentum

When Cloe's picture was to Venus shown,
Surpris'd, the goddess took it for her own.
And what, said she, does this bold painter
   mean ?
When was I bathing thus, and naked seen ?

Pleas'd Cupid heard, and check'd his
   mother's pride ;
" And who's blind now, mamma ? " the
   urchin cried.
" 'Tis Cloe's eye, and cheek, and lip, and
   breast :
Friend Howard's genius fancied all the rest."

e

THE DART
Thomas Carew

Oft when I look I may descry
A little face peep through that eye ;
Sure, that's the boy, which wisely chose
His throne among such beams as those,
Which, if his quiver chance to fall,
May serve for darts to kill withal.

ON A LADY, SLEEPING
From The Shamrock, 1774

When, for the world's repose, my Caelia
    sleeps,
See, Cupid hovers o'er the maid, and weeps.
Well may'st thou weep, fond boy ; thy
    power dies ;
Thou hast no Darts, when Caelia has no
    Eyes.

ON A WHITE FAN
Francis Atterbury

Flavia the least and slightest toy
Can with resistless art employ :
This fan, in meaner hands, would prove
An engine of small force in love ;
Yet she with graceful air and mien,
Not to be told, or safely seen,
Directs its wanton motion so,
That it wounds more than Cupid's bow ;
Gives coolness to the matchless dame,
To every other breast a flame.

TO A LADY, OFFERING TO TELL
THE AUTHOR HIS FORTUNE
Henry Needler

Chloe, you well my future fate may show,
Which, whether good or bad, from you
must flow.
With needless care you search the stars and
skies ;
No stars can influence me, but those bright
eyes.
The gods, that govern by supreme decree,
In their own minds may all events foresee.

A LOVER'S REFLECTION
William Popple

How shall I shake off cold despair,
And warm Amelia's breast ?
Be *bold !*—Alas, what Lover dare,
Who trembles to be blest ?

TO MADAME DU CHATELET UPON
HER VISIT TO STRAWBERRY HILL
Horace Walpole

When beauteous Helen left her native air,
Greece for ten years in arms reclaim'd the
fair ;
Th' enamour'd boy withheld his lovely prize,
And stak'd his country's ruin 'gainst her eyes.
Your charms less baneful, not less strong
appear ;
We welcome any peace that keeps you here.

ON THE DEATH OF A LADY'S CAT
William Harrison

And is Miss Tabby from the world retir'd ?
And are her lives, all her nine lives, expir'd ?
What sounds so moving, as her own, can tell
How Tabby died, how full of play she fell !
Begin, ye tuneful Nine, a mournful strife ;
For every Muse should celebrate a life.

ON A TEA CHEST OF MRS. HEBERDEN'S
MADE OF OLIVE-WOOD, WHICH WAS FOUND AT ATHENS
BY MR. STUART
—— *Tyrrwhitt*

In Attic fields, by fam'd Ilissus flood,
A tree to Pallas sacred once I stood ;
Now, torn from thence, with graceful em-
blems drest,
For Mira's tea I form a polish'd chest.
Athens, farewell—nor yet do I repine
For my Socratic shades and patroness divine.

ON FOP, A DOG BELONGING TO
LADY THROCKMORTON
August 1792
William Cowper

Though once a puppy, and though Fop by
name,
Here moulders one whose bones some
honour claim ;
No sycophant, although of spaniel race,
And though no hound, a martyr to the chase.

Ye squirrels, rabbits, leverets, rejoice !
Your haunts no longer echo to his voice ;
This record of his fate exulting view,
He died worn out with vain pursuit of you.
" Yes,"—the indignant shade of Fop
    replies—
" And, worn with vain pursuit, man also
    dies."

SABINA
William Congreve

See, see, she wakes, Sabina wakes !
   And now the sun begins to rise ;
Less glorious is the morn that breaks
   From his bright beams, than her fair eyes.

With light united, day they give,
   But different fates ere night fulfil ;
How many by his warmth will live !
   How many will her coldness kill !

TO MIRA AT A REVIEW
Lord Lansdowne

Let meaner beauties conquer singly still,
But haughty Mira will by thousands kill ;
Through well-arm'd ranks triumphantly she
    drives,
And with one glance commands a thousand
    lives :
The trembling heroes nor resist nor fly,
But at the head of all their squadrons die.

WRITTEN   ON   AN   HOUR-GLASS
Josiah Relph : from the Latin of Amaltheus

These little atoms that in silence pour,
And measure out with even pace the hour,
Were once Alcippus ; struck by Galla's eyes,
Wretched he burnt, and here in ashes lies :
Which ever streaming this sad truth attest,
" That lovers count the time, and know no
    rest."

AN OATH
Sir A. T. Quiller-Couch

A month ago Lysander pray'd
    To Jove, to Cupid, and to Venus,
That he might die if he betray'd
    A single vow that pass'd between us.

Ah, careless gods, to hear so ill
    And cheat a maid on you relying !
For false Lysander's thriving still,
    And 'tis Corinna lies a-dying.

OF A LADY WHO WRIT IN PRAISE
OF MYRA
Edmund Waller

While she pretends to make the graces known
Of matchless Myra, she reveals her own :
And when she would another's praise indite,
Is by her glass instructed how to write.

INSCRIBED ON A BEAUTIFUL
GROTTO NEAR THE WATER

Thomas Warton : imitated from the Greek

The Graces sought, in yonder stream,
    To cool the fervid day,
When Love's malicious godhead came,
    And stole their robes away.

Proud of the theft, the little God
    Their robes bade Delia wear :
While they ashamed to stir abroad
    Remain all naked here.

IMITATION OF A FRENCH AUTHOR

Sir Samuel Garth

Can you count the silver lights
That deck the skies, and cheer the nights ;
Or the leaves that strow the vales,
When groves are stript by winter gales ;
Or the drops that in the morn
Hang with transparent pearl the thorn ;
Or bridegroom's joys, or miser's cares,
Or gamester's oaths, or hermit's prayers ;
Or envy's pangs, or love's alarms,
Or Marlborough's acts, or Wharton's
    charms ?

WRITTEN FOR THE TOASTING-
GLASSES OF THE KIT-CAT CLUB
TO LADY HYDE

Sir Samuel Garth

The god of wine grows jealous of his art,
He only fires the head, but Hyde the heart.
The queen of love looks on, and smiles to
    see
A nymph more mighty than a deity.

WRITTEN FOR THE SAME
TO THE DUCHESS OF S. ALBANS

Earl of Halifax

The line of Vere, so long renown'd in arms,
Concludes with lustre in S. Albans' charms.
Her conquering eyes have made their race
    complete :
They rose in valour, and in beauty set.

WRITTEN FOR THE SAME
TO THE LADY MANCHESTER

Joseph Addison

While haughty Gallia's dames, who spread
O'er their pale cheeks an artful red,
Beheld this beauteous stranger there
In native charms, divinely fair,
Confusion in their looks they show'd,
And with unborrow'd blushes glow'd.

THE LADY WHO OFFERS HER
LOOKING-GLASS TO VENUS

Matthew Prior : imitated from Ausonius

Venus, take my votive glass ;
Since I am not what I was,
What from this day I shall be,
Venus, let me never see.

LAIS OLD

After the same original as the above

from Orlando Gibbons' 1st set of madrigals,
1612

Lais, now old, that erst all-tempting lass,
To Goddess Venus consecrates her glass ;
For she herself hath now no use of one,
No dimpled cheeks hath she to gaze upon :
She cannot see her springtide damask grace,
Nor dare she look upon her winter face.

UNDER A LADY'S PICTURE

Edmond Waller

Such Helen was ; and who can blame the boy
That in so bright a flame consum'd his
Troy ?
But had like virtue shin'd in that fair Greek,
The am'rous shepherd had not dared to seek
Or hope for pity, but with silent moan,
And better fate, had perishèd alone.

CELIA
Josiah Relph

For Phœbus' aid my voice I raise
  To make the charms of Celia known,
But Phœbus cannot bear to praise
  A face that's brighter than his own.

ON SOME SNOW THAT MELTED ON
A LADY'S BREAST
From Steele's Miscellany, 1714

Those envious flakes came down in haste,
  To prove her breast less fair ;
Grieving to find themselves surpass'd,
  Dissolv'd into a tear.

A COMPLAINT AGAINST CUPID
William Cartwright

Venus, redress a wrong that's done
By that young sprightful boy, thy son.
He wounds, and then laughs at the sore—
Hatred itself could do no more.
If I pursue, he's small and light,
Both seen at once, and out of sight :
If I do fly, he's winged, and then,
At the first step, I'm caught agen :
Lest one day thou thyself mayst suffer so,
Or clip the wanton's wings, or break his bow.

VENUS GENETRIX
MRS. W——N, 1760
Richard Graves

When Stella joins the blooming throng
  Of virgins dancing on the plain,
A Grace she seems the nymphs among,
  Or Dian 'midst her virgin train.

But when with sweet maternal air
  She leads Iulus through the grove,
Herself appears like Venus fair,
  Her wanton boy the god of love.

WHY I WRITE NOT OF LOVE
Ben Jonson

Some act of Love's bound to rehearse,
I thought to bind him in my verse :
Which when he felt, Away, quoth he,
Can poets hope to fetter me ?
It is enough, they once did get
Mars and my mother, in their net :
I wear not these my wings in vain.
With which he fled me ; and again
Into my rhymes could ne'er be got
By any art : then wonder not,
That since, my numbers are so cold,
When Love is fled, and I grow old.

DESTRUCTION

Josiah Relph : from Anacreon

You the fate of Phrygia's town
Sing, my friend ; and I my own :
Me no ships that cross'd the main,
Me nor horse nor foot have slain ;
But an army strange that lies
Skulking in Aurelia's eyes.

SPOKEN EXTEMPORE TO A LADY

ON WEARING AN ORANGE-COLOURED BREAST-KNOT*

John St. Ledger

Thou little Tory ! why the jest
Of wearing orange in thy breast ?
When that same breast betraying shows
The whiteness of the Rebel Rose.

* The lady was Miss Ambrose, a celebrated Irish beauty.

I have given the epigram as it appears—anonymously—in the *Curious Miscellany* (Dublin, 1749), brought to my notice by Mr. I. A. Williams. This is no doubt the original text : Miss Ambrose subscribed for twenty copies of the book. As regards the authorship, I agree with Mr. Williams in following the authority of the *Asylum for Fugitive Pieces*, 1785, for I have found no confirmation of the ascription to Lord Chesterfield : but it is unsatisfactory not to know who John St. Ledger was.

ON A YOUNG LADY OF THE NORTH

*John Whaley : from the Latin of Dr.
Timothy Thomas*

Though from the North the damsel came,
  All Spring is in her breast ;
Her skin is of the driven snow,
  But sunshine all the rest.

CUPID'S DEFEAT

William Browne

Lo, Cupid leaves his bow. His reason is,
Because your eyes wound when his shafts
    do miss.

THE WHITE ROSE

(LINES SUPPOSED TO HAVE BEEN SENT BY THE DUKE
OF CLARENCE, OF THE HOUSE OF YORK, WITH A WHITE
ROSE TO LADY ELIZA BEAUCHAMP, OF THE HOUSE OF
LANCASTER.)

*William Somerville. (Stanza II? William
Congreve)*

If this pale rose offend thy sight,
  It in thy bosom wear,
'Twill blush to find itself less white,
  And turn Lancastrian there.

But if thy ruby lip it spy,
  To kiss it shouldst thou deign,
With envy pale 'twill lose its dye,
  And Yorkist turn again.

ON THE BIRTH OF A FRIEND'S CHILD

Ernest Dowson

Mark the day white, on which the Fates have
    smiled :
Eugenio and Egeria have a child.
On whom abundant grace kind Jove imparts
If she but copy either parent's parts.
Then, Muses ! long devoted to her race,
Grant her Egeria's virtues and her face ;
Nor stop your bounty there, but add to it
Eugenio's learning and Eugenio's wit.

A MOTHER'S VOW TO ARTEMIS AFTER CHILDBIRTH

Walter Leaf : from the Greek of Callimachus

Come yet once more, Lucina, when I pray,
    To soothe a mother's pain in mother's
       joy ;
This gift is for a girl ; may one some day
    Adorn thy fragrant temple for a boy.

§ III

MAINLY CRITICAL

∽―――――――――――――∽

EPIGRAMS OF AN ANTHOLOGIST

George R. Hamilton

(I) THE JESTING EPITAPH

" The fools," cried Death, " they shall not
    laugh,"
And smashed, with one blow, tomb and
    epitaph. . . .
But Tom the offending verse had took
And put it safely in a little book,
And Death felt in a weak position,
Hearing the magnitude of Tom's edition.

(II) ART AND NATURE

ON THE INDECENT EPIGRAMS OF
HENRY PARROT (fl. 1613)

The noble Milton heard the speech of Hell
And made it Heaven's by his potent spell ;
No less a hearer, this ignoble bird
In tones exact repeated what it heard.

(III) EPITAPH ON AN EPIGRAM

Here an epigram doth lie
In this tome's obscurity.
When 'twas born, it was a jest
Pleas'd its father's mind the best ;
When (for sickly 'twas) it died,
He, with still-surviving pride,
Did to help the printers call
And gave 't a public funeral :
Since when it rests, without a date,
Beneath deep dust, inviolate.

TO PLAYWRIGHT
Ben Jonson

Playwright me reads, and still my verses
damns,
He says I want the tongue of epigrams ;
I have no salt, no bawdry he doth mean ;
For witty, in his language, is obscene.
Playwright, I loathe to have thy manners
known
In my chaste book ; profess them in thine
own.

TO THE PRODUCER OF A RECENT LIGHT MUSICAL ENTERTAINMENT
WHO BOASTED OF ITS COST
J. B. Priestley

If you paid thirty thousand for this stuff,
Flesh must be dear, for dirt is cheap enough.

TO G. S. ESQ., F.R.S.
Richard Graves

Give me the thing that's pretty, odd, and new :
All ugly, old, odd things I leave to you.

ON THE FRONTISPIECE TO THE
"DUNCIAD"

From the Daily Gazetteer, 1738*

Pallas for wisdom priz'd her fav'rite owl ;
Pope for its dulness chose the self-same fowl :
Which shall we praise, or which shall we
    despise ?
If Pope is witty, Pallas is not wise !

APOLLO'S REVENGE ON DAPHNE
*From certain Epigrams in Laud and Praise
of the Gentlemen of the Dunciad. N.D.*

When Phœbus gave the skittish Daphne chase,
And grasp'd a tree in his deceiv'd embrace ;
The god, in pique prophetic, thus express'd
His certain vengeance, and the nymph
    address'd :
Thou hast, fair vegetable, 'scap'd my pow'r,
But to that form art chang'd in luckless hour ;
Since thy coy pride the god of wit declin'd,
Thy leaves still curst shall witless temples
    bind.

* According to *Notes and Queries*, 2nd S., II,
182. It appears, however, overweighted by four additional lines, in *A Collection of Epigrams* (2nd
edition), Vol. II, 1737.

f

FROM THE FRENCH
Sir William Watson

Says Marmontel, The secret's mine
Of Racine's art-of-verse divine.
To do thee justice, Marmontel,
Never was secret kept so well.

TO A BIBLIOMANIAC
Edmund Gosse : paraphrased from Ausonius

Because your books are richly bound,
  You feel a scholar through and through ?
Then one Cremona, smooth and sound,
  Might make a fiddler of you, too !

THE BOOKWORMS
Robert Burns

Through and through the inspirèd leaves,
  Ye maggots, make your windings :
But, oh ! respect his lordship's taste,
  And spare his golden bindings !

ON GEORGE II. AND COLLEY CIBBER
Samuel Johnson

Augustus still survives in Maro's strain,
And Spenser's verse prolongs Eliza's reign ;
Great George's acts let tuneful Cibber sing,
For Nature form'd the Poet for the King.

ON DIDACTICS IN POETRY
Austin Dobson

Parnassus' peaks still catch the sun ;
 But why—O lyric brother !—
Why build a Pulpit on the one,
 A Platform on the other ?

MR. GREATHEED AND HIS TRAGEDY
From An Asylum for Fugitive Pieces, 1785

Cries Greatheed " if my meaning few can
  tell,
 My words, at least, are such as Shakespeare wrote " :
Thus senseless, drunken Steph'no, in his
  cell,
 Leaves Prospero's wand, and steals his
  old great coat.

BATHO
Aubrey de Vere

With Clio's aid old Homer sang, 'tis known :
When Batho sings, the merit's all his own.

ON ELPHINSTONE'S TRANSLATION OF MARTIAL'S EPIGRAMS
Robert Burns

O thou whom Poetry abhors,
Whom Prose has turnèd out of doors,
Heard'st thou that groan—proceed no
  further,
'Twas laurell'd Martial roaring murther.

EPITAPH FOR SIR ISAAC NEWTON
Alexander Pope

Nature and Nature's laws lay hid in night ;
God said, *Let Newton be*, and all was light.

UNDER MR. MILTON'S PICTURE, BEFORE HIS PARADISE LOST
John Dryden

Three Poets, in three distant ages born,
Greece, Italy, and England did adorn.
The first, in loftiness of thought surpass'd ;
The next, in majesty ; in both the last.
The force of nature could no farther go ;
To make a third, She join'd the other two.

VERSES WRITTEN IN SYLVIA'S "PRIOR"
David Garrick

Untouch'd by love, unmov'd by wit,
    I found no charms in Matthew's lyre,
But unconcern'd read all he writ,
    Though Love and Phœbus did inspire :

Till Sylvia took her favourite's part,
    Resolv'd to prove my judgment wrong ;
Her proofs prevail'd, they reach'd my heart,
    And soon I felt the poet's song.

ON GARRICK AND BARRY IN THE CHARACTER OF KING LEAR

Richard Kendal

The town has found out different ways
    To praise its different Lears.
To Barry it gives loud huzzas,
    To Garrick only tears.

A king ? Aye, every inch a king—
    Such Barry doth appear :
But Garrick's quite another thing ;
    He's every inch King Lear.

IN THE EXHIBITION, 1805

William Lisle Bowles

What various objects strike with various
    force,
Achilles, Hebe, and Sir Watkin's horse !
Here summer scenes, there Pentland's
    stormy ridge,
Lords, ladies, Noah's ark, and Cranford
    Bridge !
Some that display the elegant design,
The lucid colours, and the flowing line ;
Some that might make, alas ! Walsh Porter*
    stare,
And wonder how the devil they got there !

* "A gentleman well known for his taste and fine collection." (*Note in Poetical Works*, 1855.)

FUGITIVE PIECES
W. S. Landor

Fugitive pieces ! no, indeed,
How can they be whose feet are lead ?

TO AN OBSCURE EPIGRAMMATIST
Alexander Robertson of Struan

Thy thoughts in deep obscurity to fetter,
Write not at all, thy silence does it better.

THE POETASTER
J. St. Loe Strachey

Rewrite the thrice rewritten. Strive to say
Some older nothing in some newer way.

LINES IN RIDICULE OF CERTAIN POEMS PUBLISHED IN 1777
Samuel Johnson

Wheresoe'er I turn my view,
All is strange, yet nothing new ;
Endless labour all along,
Endless labour to be wrong ;
Phrase that time hath flung away,
Uncouth words in disarray,
Trick'd in antique ruff and bonnet,
Ode and elegy and sonnet.

THE CONVERSE

Matthew Prior

Yes, every poet is a fool :
  By demonstration Ned can show it :
Happy, could Ned's inverted rule
  Prove every fool to be a poet.

ON ONE WHO MADE LONG EPITAPHS

Alexander Pope

Freind, for your epitaphs I'm griev'd,
  Where still so much is said ;
One half will never be believ'd,
  The other never read.

BURLESQUE

Samuel Johnson

If the man who turnips cries,
Cry not when his father dies,
'Tis a proof that he had rather
Have a turnip than his father.

FASHIONS IN POETRY

W. S. Landor

The *Swain* and *Nymph* went out together,
Now *Knight* and *Ladie* ride o'er heather :
And who come next ? Perhaps again
Will smirk and sidle *Nymph* and *Swain*.

TO A LIVING AUTHOR
From the Poetical Register, Vol. 2 (1803)
Your comedy I've read, my friend,
    And like the half you pilfer'd best ;
Be sure the piece you yet may mend—
    Take courage, man, and steal the rest.

TO A PLAGIARIST
James Davies : from Janus Pannonius
Pirating Virgil, thou art apt to use
His loans on Homer as a fair excuse.
Quit shalt thou be : nay, placed on poet-
    roll,
If only thou wilt steal as Virgil stole.

ON A GREAT PLAGIARIST
Aubrey de Vere
Phœbus drew back with just disdain
    The wreath : the Delphic Temple
        frowned :
The suppliant fled to Hermes' fane,
    That stood on lower, wealthier ground.

The Thief-God spake, with smile star-
        bright :
" Go thou where luckier poets browse
The pastures of the Lord of Light,
    And do—what I did with his cows."*

* He stole, killed, and ate the whole of Apollo's
herd before he was a day old. (See Homer's *Hymn to
Mercury*.)

THE WRITER
Hildebrand Jacob

Titus reads neither prose nor rhyme ;
He writes himself ; he has no time.

EPIGRAM AND EPIC
Richard Garnett

Fired with the thirst of Fame, thus honest
    Sam,
" I will arise and write an epigram."
An epic, Sam, more glorious still would be,
And much more easily achieved by thee.

TO CERTAIN MODERN THEORISTS
J. B. Priestley

He who confounds the young gods with the
    brutes,
    The origin, not end, his single care,
May he be given naught but earthy roots,
    When next he calls for apple, plum or pear.

A CURE FOR POETRY
*Thomas Seward : slightly altered from John
Heywood*

Seven wealthy towns contend for Homer
    dead
Thro' which the living Homer beg'd his
    bread.

ON A STATUE OF NIOBE
From A Collection of Epigrams, 1727

To stone the Gods have chang'd her—but
  in vain ;
The Sculptor's art gave her to breathe again.

ON HOMER
From Alpheus : Spectator, No. 551

Still in our ears Andromache complains,
And still in sight the fate of Troy remains ;
Still Ajax fights, still Hector's dragg'd along,
Such strange enchantment dwells in Homer's
  song ;
Whose birth could more than one poor realm
  adorn,
For all the world is proud that he was born.

ON CATULLUS
W. S. Landor

Tell me not what too well I know
About the bard of Sirmio. . . .
    Yes, in Thalia's son
Such stains there are . . . as when a Grace
Sprinkles another's laughing face
    With nectar, and runs on.

ON A PEOPLE'S POET
Sir William Watson

Yes, threadbare seem his songs, to lettered
  ken.
They were worn threadbare next the hearts
  of men.

TO "ANON"
I. A. Williams
May Clio never come to rout you
From that kind shade around you hung :
Enough to know one thing about you—
The cadenced beauty of your tongue.

MILTON
J. B. Tabb
So fair the vision that the night
Abided with thee, lest the light,
A flaming sword before thine eyes,
Had shut thee out from Paradise.

ON DONNE'S POETRY
S. T. Coleridge
With Donne, whose muse on dromedary
    trots,
Wreathe iron pokers into true-love knots ;
Rhyme's sturdy cripple, fancy's maze and
    clue,
Wit's forge and fire-blast, meaning's press
    and screw.

ON SWIFT
Hartley Coleridge
First in the list behold the caustic Dean,
Whose muse was like himself compact of
    spleen ;
Whose sport was ireful, and his laugh severe,
His very kindness cutting, cold, austere.

CONFESSION OF JEALOUSY

W. S. Landor

Jealous, I own it, I was once,
That wickedness I here renounce.
I tried at wit . . . it would not do . . .
At tenderness . . . that fail'd me too,
Before me on each path there stood
The witty and the tender Hood.

TO ——

Sir William Watson

Forget not, brother singer ! that though
    Prose
Can never be too truthful or too wise,
Song is not Truth, not Wisdom, but the rose
    Upon Truth's lips, the light in Wisdom's
    eyes.

SCULPTURE AND SONG

Sir William Watson

The statue—Buonarrotti said—doth wait,
Thrall'd in the block, for me to liberate.
The poem—saith the poet—wanders free
Till I betray it to captivity.

TO A POET
Sir William Watson

Time, the extortioner, from richest beauty
Takes heavy toll and wrings rapacious duty.
Austere of feature if thou carve thy rhyme,
Perchance 'twill pay the lesser tax to Time.

ART
Sir William Watson

The thousand painful steps at last are trod,
　At last the temple's difficult door we win ;
But perfect on his pedestal, the god
　Freezes us hopeless when we enter in.

ON THE CONCLUSION OF A WAR
Sir William Watson

The lyre, 'tis said, in ages long ago,
Sprang from the tense string of the warrior's
　bow.
If Music thus was born of hate and pain,
O Soul of Man, so be she born again !

ON A CERTAIN POET'S DICTUM
I. A. Williams

" Life is a farce," a cynic once reflected.
" A tragedy ! " an am'rous youth corrected.
" A comedy," a quiet grey-beard said,
" To pass the time before we go to bed."

NATURE AND THE DEAD ARTIST

Eden Phillpotts

All that he needed I gave :
A cradle, a roof and a grave ;
For all that he hungered and fought,
I spared not one thought.

THE IMMORTAL RESIDUE

Adelaide Crapsey

Wouldst thou find my ashes ? Look
In the pages of my book ;
And, as these thy hand doth turn,
Know here is my funeral urn.

A DEDICATION

Herbert Asquith

Friend, if all these verses die :
Soon will you and soon will I :
But, if any word should live,
Then that word to you I give.

§ IV

MAINLY ROMANTIC

THE LOVER'S LUTE
J. C. Squire

The moonlight song Leander's love would
    hear,
The song that climbed the towers of Guine-
    vere,
Live on my lips, and I can echo yet
The song of Romeo and Juliet.
I know them all, and I by heart can say
The song of Troilus to Cressida.

UPON A GENTLEWOMAN WITH A SWEET VOICE
Robert Herrick

So long you did not sing, or touch your lute,
We knew 'twas Flesh and Blood, that there
    sat mute.
But when your playing, and your voice came
    in,
'Twas no more you then, but a *Cherubin*.

LOVE, WHAT IT IS
Robert Herrick

Love is a circle that doth restless move
In the same sweet eternity of Love.

ON HIMSELF
Robert Herrick

I dislikt but even now ;
Now I love I know not how.
Was I idle, and that while
Was I fired with a smile ?
I'll to work, or play, and then
I shall quite dislike agen.

WHEN I BEHOLD
From Dr. John Wilson's *Cheerful Airs or Ballads*, 1660

When I behold my mistress' face
Where beauty hath her dwelling-place,
And see those seeing stars, her eyes,
In whom love's fire for ever lies,
And hear her witty charming words,
Her sweet tongue to mine ear affords,
Methinks he wants wit, ears and eyes
Whom love makes not idolatrise.

ON A LADY HALF MASKING HERSELF WHEN SHE SMIL'D
Ambrose Philips

So when the Sun, with his meridian light,
Too fiercely darts upon our feeble sight ;
We thank th' officious cloud, by whose kind
   aid
We view his glory, lessen'd in a shade.

A TRINITY
Hilaire Belloc

Of Three in One and One in Three
My narrow mind would doubting be
Till Beauty, Grace and Kindness met
And all at once were Juliet.

UPON HIS MISTRESS DANCING
James Shirley

I stood, and saw my mistress dance,
    Silent, and with so fixed an eye,
Some might suppose me in a trance :
    But being askèd, Why ?
By one that knew I was in love ;
    I could not but impart
My wonder to behold her move
    So nimbly, with a marble heart.

LOVE FOUND WANTING
Patrick Hannay

Whenas I wake, I dream oft of my dear,
And oft am serious with her in my sleep ;
I am oft absent when I am most near,
And near whenas I greatest distance keep :
These wonders love doth work, but yet I
    find
That love wants power to make my Mistress
    kind.

g

THEFT OF FIRE
William Drummond

Prometheus am I,
The Heavens my Lady's eye,
From which I stealing Fire,
Find since a Vulture on my heart to tyre.

THE STATUE OF VENUS SLEEPING
William Drummond

Passenger, vex not thy mind,
To make me mine eyes unfold ;
For if thou shouldest them behold,
Thine, perhaps, they will make blind.

ON CHLORIS WALKING IN THE SNOW
William Strode

I saw fair Chloris walk alone,
When feather'd rain came softly down,
And Jove descended from his tower
To court her in a silver shower :
The wanton snow flew to her breast,
Like little birds into their nest ;
And overcome with whiteness there,
For grief it thaw'd into a tear ;
Thence falling on her garment's hem,
To deck her, froze into a gem.

LOVE VAGABONDING
William Drummond

Sweet nymphs, if as ye stray
Ye find the froth-born goddess of the sea,
All blubber'd, pale, undone,
Who seeks her giddy son,
That little god of love,
Whose golden shafts your chastest bosoms
     prove ;
Who leaving all the heavens hath run away ;
If aught to him that finds him she'll impart,
Tell her he nightly lodgeth in my heart.

A PRAYER TO SAINT ANTHONY OF PADUA
Arthur Symons

Saint Anthony of Padua, whom I bear
In effigy about me, hear my prayer :
Kind saint who findest what is lost, I pray,
Bring back her heart : I lost it yesterday.

SNOWY NIGHT
Maurice Hewlett

The snow lies deep, ice-fringes hem the
     thatch ;
I knock my shoes, my Love lifts me the latch,
Shows me her eyes—O frozen stars, they shine
Kindly ! I clasp her. Quick ! her lips are
     mine.

SELF-ESTEEM
Anna Wickham

Love with a liquid ecstasy
Did wholly fill me up,
And since his drink is sweet to me
Can I despise the cup ?

MODESTY
Aaron Hill

As lamps burn silent, with unconscious light,
So modest ease in beauty shines most bright ;
Unaiming charms with edge resistless fall,
And she, who means no mischief, does it all.

TO A LADY
George Jeffreys

Your hand and voice the judging ear delight,
And in the dance you doubly charm the sight :
Where shall we meet, but in the spheres and
    you,
So smooth a motion, and such music too !

THE WINGS OF EROS
Sir William Watson

Love, like a bird, hath perched upon a spray
    For thee and me to harken what he sings.
Contented, he forgets to fly away ;
    But hush ! . . . remind not Eros of his
    wings.

LOVE TEARS
William Cartwright

Brag not a Golden Rain, O Jove ; we see
Cupid descend in showers as well as thee.

THE PROPHET
Andrew Lang : from Antiphilus

I knew it in your childish grace
  The dawning of Desire,
" Who lives," I said, " will see that face
  Set all the world on fire ! "
They mocked ; but Time has brought to pass
  The saying over-true ;
Prophet and martyr now, alas,
  I burn for Truth,—and you !

ON LOVE
Robert Herrick

Love's of itself too sweet : the best of all
Is, when Love's honey has a dash of gall.

ON THE COUNTESS OF SOMERSET'S PICTURE
William Browne

The pity'd fortune most men chiefly hate ;
And rather think the envy'd fortunate :
Yet I, if Misery did look as She,
Should quickly fall in love with Misery.

RELEASE
Lord Nugent

Since first you knew my am'rous smart,
    Each day augments your proud disdain ;
'Twas then enough to break my heart,
    And now, thank heav'n! to break my chain.
Cease, thou scorner, cease to shun me !
    Now let love and hatred cease !
Half that rigour had undone me,
    All that rigour gives me peace.

TO AN INSCRUTABLE MISTRESS
J. C. Squire

Proud alien eyes, command me, body and
    mind,
If my surrenders can but make you kind ;
Do with me as you will, be eloquent
Of all you want from me, only relent.
In vain I plead. O pitiless lovely eyes,
The more I yield, the more you tyrannise.

KINDNESS UNKIND
John Freeman

Prone in the dark I lay, unsensed, forgot,
While over me Time's minutes fell like rain.
Then you, by whom I died, some kindness
    cast
Upon my memory, and I bled again.

EVER PRESENT

Philip Ayres

Her name is at my tongue, whene'er I speak,
　Her shape's before my eyes where'er I stir;
Both day and night, as if her ghost did walk,
　And not she me, but I had murder'd her.

DOUBLE TROUBLE

J. C. Mangan : from the Ottoman

I am blinded by thy hair and by thy tears
　together—
The dark night and the rain come down on
　me together.

TO AMINE

ON SEEING HER ABOUT TO VEIL HER MIRROR

J. C. Mangan : from the Ottoman

Veil not thy mirror, sweet Amine,
Till night shall also veil each star !
Thou seest a twofold marvel there :
The only face so fair as thine,
The only eyes that, near or far,
Can gaze on thine without despair.

ON A ROSE FOR HER BOSOM

Hilaire Belloc

Go, lovely rose, and tell the lovelier fair
That he which loved her most was never there.

THE CHANGE

Lord Nugent

I lov'd thee beautiful and kind,
   And plighted an eternal vow.
So alter'd are thy face and mind,
   'Twere perjury to love thee now.

TO CLARISSA

Lord Nugent

Why like a tyrant wilt thou reign,
When thou may'st rule the willing mind ?
Can the poor pride of giving pain
Repay the joys that wait the kind ?
I curse my fond enduring heart,
Which scorn'd presumes not to be free,
Condemn'd to feel a double smart,
To hate myself, and burn for thee.

TO HIS FALSE MISTRESS

William Walsh

Thou saidst that I alone thy heart could
   move,
And that for me thou wouldst abandon Jove.
I lov'd thee then, nor with a love defil'd,
But as a father loves his only child.
I know thee now, and though I fiercelier burn,
Thou art become the object of my scorn.
See what thy falsehood gets ; I must confess
I love thee more, but I esteem thee less.

A DIVIDED MIND
A. J. Butler : from Philodemus

My heart forewarns me to forsake the quest,
Knowing the olden tears and ruined rest.
Forsake the quest I cannot : love returns :
My heart forewarns, but warns me false—
     and burns.

THE APPARITION
Stephen Phillips

My dead love came to me, and said :
   " God gives me one hour's rest
To spend upon the earth with thee :
   How shall we spend it best ? "

" Why, as of old," I said, and so
   We quarrell'd as of old.
But when I turn'd to make my peace
   That one short hour was told.

THE IDOL
Ernest Dowson

Because I am idolatrous and have besought,
With grievous supplication and consuming
     prayer,
The admirable image that my dreams have
     wrought
Out of her swan's neck and her dark, abund-
     ant hair :
The jealous gods, who brook no worship
     save their own,
Turned my live idol marble and her heart
     to stone.

THE QUESTION

Norman Gale

Lovely of hair and breast and face,
Utterly lost to Christian grace,
    How will you lift that bankrupt head
    When all the butterfly beauty's dead ?

TO ONE FALSE

W. S. Landor

Go on, go on, and love away !
Mine was, another's is, the day.
Go on, go on, thou false one ! now
Upon his shoulder rest thy brow,
And look into his eyes until
Thy own, to find them colder, fill.

INSIGHT

W. S. Landor

I held her hand, the pledge of bliss,
    Her hand that trembled and withdrew ;
She bent her head before my kiss. . . .
    My heart was sure that hers was true.
Now I have told her I must part,
    She shakes my hand, she bids adieu,
Nor shuns the kiss. Alas, my heart !
    Hers never was the heart for you.

ANTONY AT ACTIUM
Sir William Watson

He holds a dubious balance :—yet *that* scale,
Whose freight the world is, surely shall
    prevail ?
No ; Cleopatra droppeth into *this*
One counterpoising orient sultry kiss.

ON THE TOILET TABLE OF QUEEN MARIE-ANTOINETTE
J. B. B. Nichols

This was her table, these her trim outspread
Brushes and trays and porcelain cups for red ;
Here sate she, while her women tired and
    curled
The most unhappy head in all the world.

ON SEEING A HAIR OF LUCRETIA BORGIA
W. S. Landor

Borgia, thou once wert almost too august
And high for adoration ; now thou'rt dust.
All that remains of thee these plaits unfold,
Calm hair, meandering in pellucid gold.

EPITAPH
Lady Margaret Sackville

Neither of Earth nor Heaven here she lies :
Poor troubled ashes, gentle and unwise.

ON ONE WHO DIED YOUNG
Henry Needler : from Claudian

To great and beauteous things, a transient
   date
And sudden downfall is decreed by Fate :
Witness the fair, that here in silence lies,
Whom Venus might have view'd with
   envious eyes.

ON ALBINA
John Whaley : from Marullus

Here fair Albina lies, yet not alone ;
That was forbid by Cytherea's son :
His quiver, arrows, and his bow lie here,
And Beauty's self lay lifeless on her bier.
Strew roses then, and violets round her
   shower,
She, that's now dust, was yesterday a flower.

THE CURSE
Robert Herrick

Go, perjur'd man ; and if thou ere return
To see the small remainders in mine urn :
When thou shalt laugh at my religious dust ;
And ask, Where's now the colour, form and
   trust
Of Woman's beauty ? and with hand more
   rude
Rifle the flowers which the virgins strew'd :
Know, I have pray'd to Fury, that some wind
May blow my ashes up, and strike thee blind.

EPITAPH

E. L. Davison

Hereby forbear of Death to speak,
For here his fatal whisper fell
That drove the colour from my cheek
The hour I heard my wedding-bell.

AN EPITAPH

J. C. Squire

Shiftless and shy, gentle and kind and frail,
    Poor wanderer, bewildered into vice,
You are freed at last from seas you could not
        sail,
    A wreck upon the shores of Paradise.

TO STELLA

P. B. Shelley : from Plato

Thou wert the morning star among the living,
    Ere thy fair light had fled ;
Now, having died, thou art as Hesperus,
        giving
    New splendour to the dead.

DIRCE

W. S. Landor

Stand close around, ye Stygian set,
    With Dirce in one boat conveyed,
Or Charon, seeing, may forget
    That he is old and she a shade.

PROUD WORD
W. S. Landor

Proud word you never spoke, but you will
  speak
    Four not exempt from pride some future
    day.
Resting on one white hand a warm wet cheek
    Over my open volume you will say,
" This man loved *me* ! " then rise and trip
    away.

IANTHE'S QUESTION
W. S. Landor

" Do you remember me? or are you proud?"
Lightly advancing thro' her star-trimm'd
    crowd,
    Ianthe said, and lookt into my eyes.
" A *yes*, a *yes*, to both : for Memory
Where you but once have been must ever be,
    And at your voice Pride from his throne
    must rise."

THE DEMAND
W. S. Landor

Remain, ah not in youth alone,
    Tho' youth, where you are, long will stay,
But when my summer days are gone,
    And my autumnal haste away.
" *Can I be always by your side ?* "
    No, but the hours you can, you must,
Nor rise at Death's approaching stride,
    Nor go when dust is gone to dust.

LOVE AND TIME
W. S. Landor

Love flies with bow unstrung when Time
    appears,
And trembles at the assault of heavy years ;
A few bright feathers bear him on his flight
Quite beyond call, but not forgotten quite.

THE GRATEFUL HEART
W. S. Landor

The grateful heart for all things blesses ;
    Not only joy, but grief endears :
I love you for your few caresses,
    I love you for my many tears.

ON A SLEEPING FRIEND
Hilaire Belloc

Lady, when your lovely head
Droops to sink among the Dead,
And the quiet places keep
You that so divinely sleep :
Then the dead shall blessèd be
With a new solemnity.
For such Beauty so descending
Pledges them that Death is ending.
Sleep your fill—but when you wake
Dawn shall over Lethe break.

THE LAST WISH
Lord Lytton (1831-1892)

Since all that I can ever do for thee
Is to do nothing, this my prayer must be :
That thou mayst never guess nor ever see
The all-endured this nothing-done costs me

THE TORCH OF LOVE
W. S. Landor

The torch of Love dispels the gloom
Of life, and animates the tomb ;
But never let it idly flare
On gazers in the open air,
Nor turn it quite away from one
To whom it serves for moon and sun,
And who alike in night and day
Without it could not find his way.

THE STATUE
Hilaire Belloc

When we are dead, some Hunting-boy will
pass
And find a stone half-hidden in tall grass
And grey with age : but having seen that
stone
(Which was your image), ride more slowly
on.

ON A DEAD HOSTESS
Hilaire Belloc

Of this bad world the loveliest and the best
Has smiled and said " Good Night," and
    gone to rest.

DEATH OF THE DAY
W. S. Landor

My pictures blacken in their frames
    As night comes on,
And youthful maids and wrinkled dames
    Are now all one.

Death of the day ! a sterner Death
    Did worse before ;
The fairest form, the sweetest breath,
    Away he bore.

THE TEAR DENIED
W. S. Landor

Mild is the parting year, and sweet
    The odour of the falling spray ;
Life passes on more rudely fleet,
    And balmless is its closing day.
I wait its close, I court its gloom,
    But mourn that never must there fall
Or on my breast or on my tomb
    The tear that would have sooth'd it all.

h

§ V

FANCIFUL TO IMAGINATIVE

TROUT LEAPING IN THE ARUN
WHERE A JUGGLER WAS DROWNED

Charles Dalmon

His flesh and bones have long since gone,
But still the stream runs gaily on,
And still his merry ghost contrives
To juggle with his silver knives.

THE STATUE OF MEDUSA

William Drummond

Of that Medusa strange,
Who those that did her see in rocks did
    change,
No image carv'd is this ;
Medusa's self it is :
For while at heat of day
To quench her thirst she by this spring did
    stay,
Her hideous head beholding in this glass,
Her senses fail'd, and thus transformed she
    was.

THE AMBER BEAD
Robert Herrick

I saw a fly within a bead
Of amber cleanly buried.
The urn was little, but the room
More rich than Cleopatra's tomb.

ON A PET CICADA
Walter Leaf : from Aristodicus

No more, shrill cricket, in rich Alkis' court
  Is heard thy voice ; no light of sun for
    thee.
Now through the meads of Hades dost thou
    sport
  And dewy flowers of Queen Persephone.

ON AN ENGRAVED GEM
*Walter Leaf : from the Greek (ascribed to
Plato)*

This little jasper shows you oxen five,
Grazing, so true they seem to be alive,
They might have wandered ; so the ring of
    gold
Makes for the little herd a little fold.

HOPEFUL GARDENING
Norman Gale

Of bushes plant the laurel most,
  And near to miracle remain ;
For none can tell when Daphne's ghost
  Will leap to lovely flesh again.

A WORCESTERSHIRE EPITAPH*

Autumn came, and Thomas had
Plums and apples for the lad.
Now the lad to manhood grown
Remembers to set up this stone,
The soul of Thomas having flown.

THE LAST CHANCE

Andrew Lang

Within the streams, Pausanias saith,
  That down Cocytus valley flow,
Girdling the grey domain of Death,
  The spectral fishes come and go ;
The ghosts of trout flit to and fro.
  Persephone, fulfil my wish,
And grant that in the shades below
  My ghost may land the ghosts of fish.

TO CRINAGORAS OF MITYLENE

A. H. Bullen

When in Elysium I shall seek out those
Who've much delighted me in verse or
    prose,
Kindly Crinagoras, I will never rest
Until I find your shade among the Blest ;
And sure I am that you will not repel
Me who have loved you long and loved you
    well.

* I have to thank Mr. A. L. Irvine for this epitaph,
which he heard from the late A. Clutton-Brock.

A LITTLE BIRD'S EPITAPH

Martin Armstrong

Here lies a little bird :
  Once all day long
Through Martha's house was heard
  His rippled song.

Tread lightly where he lies
  Beneath this stone,
With nerveless wings, closed eyes,
  And sweet voice gone.

THE OLD POSTMAN

L. A. G. Strong

Here he sits who day by day
Tramped his quiet life away :
Knew a world but ten miles wide,
Cared not what befell outside.

Nor, his tramping at an end,
Has he need of book or friend.
Peace and comfort he can find
In the laneways of his mind.

A VERY OLD MAN

J. B. Priestley

Time has filched all from him but some
  scant show of breath,
And that but waits the casual pillaging of
  Death.

EPITAPH ON A LITTLE SLAVE GIRL
Leigh Hunt : from Martial

Underneath this greedy stone
Lies little sweet Erotion,
Whom the Fates, with hearts as cold,
Nipped away at six years old.
Thou, whoever thou may'st be,
That hast this small field after me,
Let the yearly rites be paid
To her little slender shade ;
So shall no disease or jar
Hurt thy house, or chill thy Lar ;
But this tomb be here alone
The only melancholy stone.

THE OLD MAN AND THE NEWSPAPER
J. B. Priestley

Daylong he seems to read, but as he peers
At fading print, the sheet becomes a glass,
Wherein are mirrored ghosts that smile and
        pass,
And lovely faces, dust these forty years.

PLUTO AND THE PHYSICIAN
C.: after Lucillius

When Magnus pass'd below, Dis trembling
        said,
" He comes, and will to life restore my
        dead."

HECTOR

A. J. Butler : from Aceratus

Hector, whose name through Homer's Iliad
  rings,
 Thou mighty bulwark of the god-built
  wall,
With thee the poet ends : no more he sings,
 But turns his page to silence at thy fall.

AMYNTICHUS THE GARDENER

A. J. Butler : from the Greek

Take to thy heart, dear Earth, this ancient
  wight,
 Remembering his ceaseless toil on thee :
How oft he set thee olive-stems aright,
 Or decked thee with vine-branches merrily,
Or filled with corn, and water-runnels led
 To make thee rich in garden plants and
  fruit.
So lie thou kindly on his hoary head,
 And let spring blossoms round about him
  shoot.

A REMONSTRANCE

J. B. Tabb

Sing me no more, sweet warbler, for the dart
Of joy is keener than the flash of pain :
Sing me no more, for the re-echoed strain
Together with the silence breaks my heart.

THE STARS
Philip Smyth : from Ptolemy

Though but the being of a day,
When I yon planet's course survey
    This earth I then despise—
Near Jove's eternal throne I stand,
And quaff from an immortal hand
    The nectar of the skies.

FROM THE SAME
Richard Garnett

I, rapt in scrutiny as Night unbars
The thick and mazy glories of the stars,
Though earth on Earth, no more am linked
    to her,
But sit in Jove's own hall a banqueter.

FROM THE SAME
Robert Bridges

Mortal though I bé, yea ephemeral, if but
    a moment
  I gaze up to the night's starry domain of
    heaven,
Then no longer on earth I stand ; I touch
    the Creator,
  And my lively spirit drinketh immortality.

ON HOBSON THE CARRIER
From Wit's Recreations, 1640

Hobson's not dead, but Charles the Northern
    swain
Hath sent for him, to draw his lightsome-
    wain.

CONTEMPLATION
H. T. Wade-Gery

Seeing you, everlasting stars,
I am becalmèd of my vain desires,
Well knowing, while I turn my thirsting eyes
To th' uneventful perfect skies,
How the eternal Cherubim
On contemplation feed through ages dim.

ON AN ECLIPSE OF THE MOON
W. S. Landor

Struggling, and faint, and fainter didst thou
    wane,
O Moon ! and round thee all thy starry train
Came forth to help thee, with half-open eyes,
And trembled every one with still surprise,
That the black Spectre should have dared
    assail
Their beauteous queen and seize her sacred
    veil.

ON SIR FRANCIS DRAKE
From Wit's Recreations, 1640

Sir Drake, whom well the world's end knew,
   Which thou didst compass round,
And whom both poles of heaven once saw,
   Which north and south do bound :
The stars above would make thee known,
   If men here silent were ;
The sun himself cannot forget
   His fellow-traveller.

STAR-JESSAMINE

J. B. Tabb

Discerning Star from Sister Star,
　We give to each its name ;
But ye, O countless Blossoms, are
　In fragrance and in flame
So like, that He from whom ye came
　Alone discerneth each by name.

ON WILLIAM HOLORENSHAW,
THE MATHEMATICIAN

Thomas Bancroft

Lo, in small closure of this earthly bed,
Rests he, that heav'ns vast motions measurèd,
Who having known both of the land and sky,
More than fam'd Archimed or Ptolemy,
Would further press, and like a Palmer went,
With Jacob's staff beyond the Firmament.

ON JONAS, IN THE WHALE'S BELLY

From A Curious Collection of Epitaphs, 1727

Buried I am, and yet I am not dead,
Though neither earth inclose, nor stone me
　keep,
I speak, I think, with living airs am fed,
In living tomb, and in unfathom'd deep :
What wight beside myself for shame, or
　grace,
E'er liv'd in Death, in such a tomb or place ?

ETERNITY

William Blake

He who bends to himself a Joy
Doth the wingèd life destroy ;
But he who kisses the Joy as it flies
Lives in Eternity's sunrise.

TO SILENCE

J. B. Tabb

Why the warning finger-tip
Pressed for ever on thy lip ?
To remind the pilgrim Sound
That it moves on holy ground,
In a breathing-space to be
Hushed for all eternity.

LALUS' DEATH

William Drummond

Amidst the waves profound,
Far, far from all relief,
The honest fisher Lalus, ah ! is drown'd,
Shut in this little skiff ;
The boards of which did serve him for a bier,
So that when he to the black world came
  near,
Of him no silver greedy Charon got ;
For he in his own boat
Did pass that flood, by which the gods do
  swear.

A SKULL OF ROCK-CRYSTAL IN THE BRITISH MUSEUM
Charles Dalmon

A skull of bone is gruesome to the sight ;
But here is something so akin to light
That beauty seems to shine from it and say :
" *Be not deceived by what may seem decay.*"

ON MAN
W. S. Landor

In his own image the Creator made,
   His own pure sunbeam quickened thee,
   O man !
   Thou breathing dial ! since thy day began
The present hour was ever markt with shade !

RETIREMENT
W. S. Landor

" Call me not forth," said one who sate retired
Whom Love had once, but Envy never, fired.
" I scorn the crowd : no clap of hands he
      seeks
Who walks among the stateliest of the
      Greeks."

ON HIS SEVENTY-FIFTH BIRTHDAY
W. S. Landor

I strove with none ; for none was worth my
      strife.
Nature I loved and, next to Nature, Art ;
I warmed both hands before the fire of life ;
It sinks, and I am ready to depart.

INSCRIPTION ON A ROCK HAVING
THE   LIKENESS   OF   IMMENSE
HUMAN FEATURES
Sir William Watson

The seafowls build in wrinkles of my face.
Ages ere man was, man was mock'd of me.
Kings fall, gods die, worlds crash ;—at my
    throne's base
  In showers of bright white thunder breaks
    the sea.

SEA DIRGE
Andrew Lang : from Archias of Byzantium

Crushed by the waves upon the crag was I,
  Who still must hear these waves among
    the dead,
Breaking and brawling on the promontory,
  Sleepless ; and sleepless is my weary head !
For me did strangers bury on the coast
  Within the hateful hearing of the deep,
Nor Death that lulleth all, can lull my ghost,
  One sleepless soul among the souls that
    sleep !

NAPOLEON
Walter de la Mare

" What is the world, O soldiers ?
    It is I :
I, this incessant snow,
    This northern sky ;
Soldiers, this solitude
    Through which we go
      Is I."

§ VI

MAINLY MORAL AND RELIGIOUS

⌇──────────────────────────────⌇

BIRTH AND DEATH

Sir William Jones : from the Persian

On parent knees, a naked new-born child,
Weeping thou sat'st, while all around thee
    smil'd :
So live, that sinking in thy last long sleep,
Calm thou mayst smile, while all around
    thee weep.

MATERNITY

Alice Meynell

One wept whose only child was dead,
New-born, ten years ago.
" Weep not ; he is in bliss," they said.
She answered, " Even so.

" Ten years ago was born in pain
A child, not now forlorn.
But oh, ten years ago, in vain,
A mother, a mother was born."

VANITY
A. J. Butler : from Palladas of Alexandria
Naked I reached the world at birth,
Naked I pass beneath the earth :
Why toil I, then, in vain distress,
Seeing the end is nakedness ?

ON THE LIFE OF MAN
Francis Quarles
Our life is nothing but a winter's day ;
Some only break their fasts, and so, away :
Others stay dinner, and depart full fed ;
The deepest Age but sups, and goes to bed :
He's most in debt, that lingers out the day ;
Who dies betimes, has less ; and less to pay.

IMITATED FROM THE LATIN ADRIANI MORIENTIS AD ANIMAM SUAM
Matthew Prior
Poor, little, pretty, flutt'ring thing,
Must we no longer live together ?
And dost thou prune thy trembling wing,
To take thy flight thou know'st not whither ?

Thy hum'rous vein, thy pleasing folly,
Lies all neglected, all forgot ;
And pensive, wav'ring, melancholy,
Thou dread'st and hop'st thou know'st not
    what.

IN BED

Samuel Johnson : from Isaac de Benserade

In bed we laugh, in bed we cry ;
And born in bed, in bed we die :
The near approach a bed may show
Of human bliss to human woe.

NULLA DIES SINE LINEA

From Wit's Recreations, 1640

By ever learning, Solon waxèd old,
For time, he knew, was better far than gold :
Fortune would give him gold which would
    decay,
But Fortune cannot give him yesterday.

ON A WHOLE-LENGTH PORTRAIT
OF NASH

BETWEEN THE BUSTS OF NEWTON AND POPE AT BATH

Lord Chesterfield, Stanza I : Jane Brereton,
Stanza II

Immortal Newton never spoke
    More truth than here you'll find ;
Nor Pope himself e'er penn'd a joke
    Severer on mankind.

The picture, plac'd the busts between,
    Gives satire all its strength :
Wisdom and Wit are little seen,
    While Folly glares at length.

TO HIS LITTLE CHILD FROM THE TOWER

John Hoskins

Sweet Benjamin, since thou art young,
And hast not yet the use of tongue,
Make it thy slave, while thou art free ;
Imprison it, lest it do thee.

THE GROWTH OF KNOWLEDGE

William Cowper : from the Latin of John Owen

When little more than boy in age,
I deemed myself almost a sage ;
But now seem worthier to be styled
For ignorance almost a child.

LONG AND SHORT LIFE

Edmund Waller

Circles are prais'd, not that abound
In largeness, but th' exactly round :
So life we praise that does excel,
Not in much time, but acting well.

EPIGRAM

Coventry Patmore

The learned teach that Saints in Heaven
For ever grow more young and fair.
Ah, Loveliest, here amongst us even
You must have been for ever there !

i

ON A LOOKING-GLASS

Patrick Delany

When I revolve this evanescent state,
How fleeting is its form, how short its date !
My being and my stay dependent still,
Not on my own, but on another's will ;
I ask myself, as I my image view,
Which is the real shadow of the two ?

EXTEMPORARY COUNSEL TO A YOUNG GALLANT IN A FROLIC

Anne Killigrew

As you are young, if you'll be also wise,
Danger with honour court, but broils
   despise ;
Believe you then are truly brave and bold,
To beauty when no slave, and less to gold ;
When virtue you dare own, nor think it odd,
Or ungenteel, to say " I fear a God."

INDIVIDUALITY

Winifred Lucas

How life and death for every one
   Keep each to his own counsel true !
The world he trod he leaves ; to none
   The world he knew.

ONCE
Sir William Watson

Momentous to himself as I to me
  Hath each man been that woman ever bore;
Once, in a lightning-flash of sympathy,
  I *felt* this truth, an instant, and no more.

TO A BERKELEIAN IDEALIST
Sir William Watson

If Nature be a phantasm, as thou say'st,
  A mighty figment and prodigious dream,
To reach the real and true I'll make no haste,
  More than content with worlds that only
    seem.

A DEDICATION
Richard Garnett : from Mnasalcas

The crookèd bow and arrow-spending case
Promachus hangs up in this holy place,
Phœbus, to thee. The shafts remain apart,
For each is buried in a foeman's heart.

THE MOUNTAINS IN WINTER
Frances Cornford

Unutterably far, and still, and high,
The mountains stand against the sunset sky ;
O little angry heart, against your will,
You must grow quiet here, and wise, and
    still.

MAN BLIND TO FUTURE EVENTS
Francis Fawkes : from Menander

Say not, O man ! for it becomes thee not,
" This evil shall not happen to my lot."

MORTAL COMBAT
Mary E. Coleridge

It is because you were my friend,
    I fought you as the devil fights.
Whatever fortune God may send,
    For once I set the world to rights.

And that was when I thrust you down,
    And stabb'd you twice and twice again,
Because you dared take off your crown,
    And be a man like other men.

WORD OF COUNSEL
Sarah Piatt

Others will kiss you while your mouth is red.
    Beauty is brief. Of all the guests who come
While the lamp shines on flowers, and wine,
        and bread,
    In time of famine who will spare a crumb ?

Therefore, oh, next to God, I pray you keep
    Yourself as your own friend, the tried, the
        true.
Sit your own watch—others will surely sleep.
    Weep your own tears. Ask none to die
        with you.

FORTUNE
Lord Lansdowne

When Fortune seems to smile, 'tis then I
    fear
Some lurking ill, and hidden mischief near ;
Us'd to her frowns, I stand upon my guard,
And arm'd in virtue, keep my soul prepared.
Fickle and false to others she may be,
I can complain but of her constancy.

WOMEN AND MULTITUDES
Anna Wickham

When a weak knave commanded me,
Then I was stung to mutiny !
But when my king spoke his behest,
In quick obedience I found rest.
Now to the dark I cry my need,
" God send us kings, to love, and lead."

THE SONG OF PRIDE
Anna Wickham

We are unwilling to lie low,
Crushed by a cursèd tyrant " No."
Give us a fight where we can cry, " I can ! "
To show there is the seed of God in man.
If God shall strike us for our pride
Know that in joy of death we died.

CREATRIX
Anna Wickham

Let us thank Almighty God
For the woman with the rod.
Who was ever and is now
Strong essential as the plough.
She shall goad and she shall drive,
So to keep man's soul alive.
Amoris with her scented dress
Beckons, in pretty wantonness ;
But the wife drives, nor can man tell
What hands so urge, what powers compel.

LOVE
John Taylor

Love is a dying life, a living death,
A vapour, shadow, bubble and a breath :
An idle bauble, and a paltry toy,
Whose greatest patron is a blinded boy :
But pardon, Love, my judgment is unjust,
For what I spake of love, I meant of lust.

THE ATTAINMENT
Coventry Patmore

You love ? That's high as you shall go ;
    For 'tis as true as Gospel text,
Not noble then is never so
    Either in this world or the next.

A TRUTH

Coventry Patmore

'Tis truth (although this truth's a star
  Too deep-enskied for all to see),
As poets of grammar, lovers are
  The fountains of morality.

CONSTANCY REWARDED

Coventry Patmore

I vow'd unvarying faith, and she,
  To whom in full I pay that vow,
Rewards me with variety
  Which men who change can never know.

MARRIAGE INDISSOLUBLE

Coventry Patmore

" In heaven none marry." Grant the most
  Which may by this dark word be meant,
Who shall forbid the eternal boast
  " I kiss'd, and kiss'd with her consent! "
If here, to Love, past favour is
  A present boast, delight, and chain,
What lacks of honour, bond, and bliss,
  Where Now and Then are no more twain !

PLAYS
W. S. Landor

Alas, how soon the hours are over
Counted us out to play the lover !
And how much narrower is the stage
Allotted us to play the sage !
But when we play the fool, how wide
The theatre expands ! beside,
How long the audience sits before us !
How many prompters ! what a chorus !

CHOICE OF THREE
Lord Oxford

Were I a king, I could command content ;
Were I obscure, hidden should be my cares ;
Or were I dead, no cares should me torment,
Nor hopes, nor hates, nor loves, nor griefs,
    nor fears.
A doubtful choice,—of these three which to
    crave ;
A kingdom, or a cottage, or a grave.

FATUM SUPREMUM
From Wit's Recreations, 1640

All buildings are but monuments of death,
All clothes but winding sheets for our last
    knell,
All dainty fattings for the worms beneath,
All curious music but our passing bell ;
Thus death is nobly waited on, for why ?
All that we have is but death's livery.

ON A GARDENER

From Wit's Recreations, 1640

Could he forget his death that every hour
Was emblem'd to it, by the fading flower ?
Should he not mind his end ? Yes, sure he
    must,
That still was conversant 'mong beds of dust.

MY OWN EPITAPH

John Gay

Life is a jest, and all things show it ;
I thought so once, but now I know it.

SENEX TO MATT. PRIOR

J. K. Stephen

Ah ! Matt. : old age has brought to me
Thy wisdom, less thy certainty :
The world's a jest, and joy's a trinket :
I knew that once : but now—I think it.

EPITAPH FOR HIMSELF

Matthew Prior

Nobles and Heralds, by your leave,
  Here lies what once was Matthew Prior,
The son of Adam and of Eve ;
  Can Bourbon or Nassau go higher ?

THE PRIZE

Norman Gale

Sinewy Life and sinewy Death
　Stayed tug-of-war, to get their breath.
Sudden they glimpsed me ; and their eyes,
　Caught unprepared, revealed the prize.

THE FAIR

Eden Phillpotts

The fair is a fight ; some are fighting for gain ;
Some fighting for pleasure and some to cheat
　　pain ;
But that squinting old hag, with a voice like
　　a knife
And a tray of wire spiders—she's fighting for
　　life.

A DIAMOND SPEAKS

Norman Gale

He who tore me from the earth choked
　　graveward in despair ;
　He who stabbed his mate for me, hemp
　　got him by the throat !
She who paid with lovely limbs to buy me
　　for her hair
　Huddles in the rubbish at the bottom of
　　the moat.

STONE FOR A STATUE

To a Sculptor

Sarah Piatt

Leave what is white for whiter use.
　For such a purpose as your own
Would be a dreary jest, a coarse abuse,
　A bitter wrong to snowy stone.

Let the pure marble's silence hold
　Its unshaped gods, and do not break
Those hidden images divine and old,
　To-day, for one mean man's small sake !

ON THE WORLD

Francis Quarles

The World's a book, writ by th' eternal art
Of the great Maker, printed in Man's heart ;
'Tis falsely printed, though divinely penned,
And all th' Errata will appear at th' end.

ON INVALIDS

Philip Smyth : from Lucillius

For those, whom Death's unerring dart
Has reach'd, no more my tears shall flow :
But he with sorrow wrings my heart,
Who waits each hour the menac'd blow.

FATHER DAMIEN

J. B. Tabb

O God, the cleanest offering
    Of tainted earth below,
Unblushing to Thy feet we bring—
    " *A leper white as snow !* "

ULTIMATE

G. K. Chesterton

The vision of a haloed host
    That weep around an empty throne ;
And, aureoles dark and angels dead,
    Man with his own life stands alone.

" I am," he says his bankrupt creed ;
    " I am," and is again a clod :
The sparrow starts, the grasses stir,
    For he has said the name of God.

AFFLICTIONS BENEFICIAL

Samuel Sheppard

It is not for our good, in ease to rest ;
Man (like to Cassia) when bruis'd is best.

A PARADOX

Thomas Jordan

Our God requireth the whole heart, or none,
And yet He will accept a broken one.

COSMOPOLITANS

From Epigrams Sacred and Moral, 1864 :
by A. G. W.

Citizens of the world are some ;
And others of the world to come.

REPENTANCE

Francis Quarles

'Tis not to cry out mercy, or to sit
And droop, or to confess that thou hast fail'd ;
'Tis to bewail the sins thou didst commit,
And not commit the sins thou hast bewail'd :
He that bewails, and not forsakes them too,
Confesses rather what he means to do.

ANGELS OF PAIN

J. B. Tabb

Ah, should they come revisiting the spot
    Whence by our prayers we drove them
        utterly,
    Shame were it for their saddened eyes to
        see
How soon their visitations are forgot.

IDOLATRY

John Byrom

To own a God who does not speak to men,
Is first to own and then disown again :
Of all idolatry the total sum
Is having gods that are both deaf and dumb.

FROM THE LATIN

John Leyden

Once in the keen pursuit of fame
   I, schoolboy-like, pursued a bubble ;
But Death, before I gain'd a name,
   Stept in, and saved a world of trouble.

DIFFERING SORROWS

Mary E. Coleridge

Two differing sorrows made these eyes grow
   dim :
   Woe, for which all must weep, while weep
     they can,
And that more poignant anguish known to him
   Whose grief's the jest of every other man.

DEATH

Thomas MacDonagh

Life is a boon—and death, as spirit and flesh
   are twain :
The body is spoil of death, the spirit lives
   on death-free ;
The body dies and its wound dies and the
   mortal pain ;
The wounded spirit lives, wounded im-
   mortally.

DANGER OF DELAYED REPENTANCE

Henry Delaune

Cheat not yourselves as most ; who then
  prepare
  For death, when life is almost turn'd to
  fume.
One thief was sav'd, that no man might
  despair :
  And but one thief that no man might
  presume.

BEWARE!

Francis Quarles

Be sad, my heart ! deep dangers wait thy
  mirth ;
Thy soul's waylaid by sea, by hell, by earth :
Hell has her hounds ; earth, snares ; the sea,
  a shelf ;
But, most of all, my heart, beware thyself.

RESPICE FINEM

Francis Quarles

My soul, sit thou a patient looker-on ;
Judge not the play before the play is done :
Her plot hath many changes ; every day
Speaks a new scene ; the last act crowns the
  play.

THE LONG SLEEP
Sir Walter Raleigh : after Catullus

The sun may set and rise ;
But we, contrariwise,
Sleep after our short light
One everlasting night.

DEATH'S WHISPER
W. S. Landor

Death stands above me, whispering low
I know not what into my ear :
Of his strange language all I know
Is, there is not a word of fear.

THE ONE WAY
W. S. Landor

Various the roads of life ; in one
All terminate, one lonely way.
We go ; and " Is he gone ? "
Is all our best friends say.

THE TERM OF DEATH
Sarah Piatt

Between the falling leaf and rosebud's
breath ;
The bird's forsaken nest and her new song
(And this is all the time there is for Death) ;
The worm and butterfly,—it is not long !

ANONYMOUS

J. B. Tabb

Anonymous—nor needs a name
To tell the secret whence the flame,
With light, and warmth, and incense, came
A new creation to proclaim.

So was it when, His labour done,
God saw His work, and smiled thereon ;
His glory in the picture shone,
But name upon the canvas, none.

NATURE

J. B. Tabb

It is His garment ; and to them
Who touch in faith its utmost hem
He, turning, says again, " I see
That virtue hath gone out of me."

COCK-CROW

Robert Herrick

Bell-man of Night, if I about shall go
For to deny my Master, do thou crow.
Thou stop'st S. Peter in the midst of sin ;
Stay me, by crowing, ere I do begin ;
Better it is, premonish'd, for to shun
A sin, than fall to weeping when 'tis done.

k

TO ONE WHO HASTENED HEAVENWARD

Wilfrid Meynell

Ah, if too anxious for the end,
You risk the reaching of it, friend !
The runner who shall win the race
Is careful not to force the pace ;
Christ is the way : and so Saints even
Love lingering on the road to Heaven.

TWO WENT UP INTO THE TEMPLE TO PRAY

Richard Crashaw

Two went to pray ? oh, rather say
One went to brag, the other to pray.
One stands up close, and treads on high,
Where the other dares not lend his eye.
One nearer to God's altar trod ;
The other to the altar's God.

HEAVEN AND HELL

Francis Thompson

'Tis said there were no thought of hell,
　Save hell were taught; that there should be
A Heaven for all's self-credible.
　Not so the thing appears to me.
'Tis Heaven that lies beyond our sights,
　And hell too possible that proves ;
For all can feel the God that smites
　But ah, how few the God that loves !

ON THE BAPTISED ÆTHIOPIAN

ACTS VIII

Richard Crashaw

Let it no longer be a forlorn hope
   To wash an Æthiope :
He's washt, his gloomy skin a peaceful shade
   For his white soul is made ;
And now, I doubt not, the Eternal Dove
   A black-fac'd house will love.

ON THE BLESSED VIRGIN'S BASHFULNESS

Richard Crashaw

That on her lap she casts her humble eye,
'Tis the sweet pride of her humility.
The fair star is well fix'd, for where, O where
Could she have fix'd it on a fairer sphere ?
'Tis Heaven, 'tis Heaven she sees, Heaven's
    God there lies
She can see Heaven, and ne'er lift up her
    eyes :
This new Guest to her eyes new laws hath
    given,
'Twas once *look up*, 'tis now *look down* to
    Heaven.

THE CHRIST-CHILD

Mary E. Coleridge

I saw a stable, low and very bare,
  A little child in a manger.
The oxen knew Him, had Him in their care,
  To men He was a stranger.
The safety of the world was lying there,
  And the world's danger.

DORMITIO B. M. VIRGINIS

Frederick Reynolds

Thou liest, Death! It was no shaft of thine
That urged the spirit from so sweet a shrine :
But her pure heart in Love's seraphic heat
Rapt up to God's own Heart—forgot to beat!

ON THE PASSION OF CHRIST

From A Curious Collection of Epitaphs, 1727

What rends the temple's vail ? Where is
    day gone ?
How can a general darkness cloud the sun ?
Astrologers their skill in vain do try ;
Nature must needs be sick, when God can
    die.

§ VII

EPITAPHS

TO THE BABE NIVA
J. B. Tabb

Niva, Child of Innocence,
   Dust to dust *we* go :
Thou, when Winter wooed thee hence,
   Wentest snow to snow.

UPON A VIRGIN
Robert Herrick

Here a solemn fast we keep,
While all beauty lies asleep.
Hushed be all things, no noise here,
But the toning of a tear :
Or the sigh of such as bring
Cowslips for her covering.

ON A YOUNG MOTHER OF MANY CHILDREN
Robert Herrick

Let all chaste Matrons, when they chance
      to see
My num'rous issue, praise, and pity me.
Praise me, for having such a fruitful womb ;
Pity me too, who found so soon a tomb.

UPON A CHILD
Robert Herrick

Here a pretty baby lies
Sung asleep with lullabies ;
Pray be silent, and not stir
Th' easy earth that covers her.

ON A CHILD
From Camden's Remains, 1623

As careful nurses on their beds do lay
Their babes, which would too long (the
    wantons) play,
So to prevent my youth's ensuing crimes,
Nature, my nurse, laid me to bed betimes.

ON A CHILD
From Wit's Recreations, 1640

Into this world as stranger to an Inn,
This child came guest-wise, where when it
    had been
A while, and found nought worthy of his stay,
He only broke his fast, and went away.

OF A NEW-BORN BABE DYING
John Donne, the younger

I died as soon as in the world I came,
Depriv'd of baptism and without a name.
In Book of Life then nameless me record,
For my hope's only in Thy Name (O Lord).

THE JEWEL
From Wit's Recreations, 1640

In this marble casket lies
A matchless jewel of rich price ;
Whom Nature in the world's disdain
But showed, and put it up again.

ON A CHILD
From Wit's Recreations, 1640

Tread softly passenger ! for here doth lie
A dainty jewel of sweet infancy :
A harmless babe, that only came and cried
In baptism to be washt from sin and died.

ON THE DEATH OF AN INFANT LADY
Thomas Jordan

Ladies that are young and wise,
    Shall I tell ye of a Prize ?
Here a Box of Beauty lies.

A Jewel hid from vulgar view,
    Whose excellency if you knew,
Your eyes would drop like morning dew.

Dame Nature's Diamond, which when
    She saw it was too bright for men,
Shew'd it, and shut it up agen.

ON MISTRESS ANNE PRIDEAUX
WHO DIED AT THE AGE OF SIX
William Browne

Nature in this small volume was about
To perfect what in woman was left out ;
Yet fearful lest a piece so well begun
Might want preservatives, when she had
    done ;
Ere she could finish what she undertook,
Threw dust upon it, and shut up the book.

IN MEMORY OF MISS MILDRED
HANWAY, THE AUTHOR'S NIECE

John Hanway

Stay, traveller, and here suppose
Laid in the dust a lovely rose :
Whose bloom (alas each flower's fate !)
Was sweet, but of too short a date.
Fresh roses then, and lilies fling
O'er her, that has no second Spring ;
And strew 'em yearly o'er her urn,
For this sweet flow'r can ne'er return.

ON AN INFANT
Elizabeth Carter

Though infant years no pompous honours
    claim,
The vain parade of monumental fame,
To better praise the last great day shall rear
The spotless innocence that slumbers here.

ON MISTRESS ROWLAND

WHO WAS HAPPY IN HER MIND, AND LOVELY IN HER
PERSON : BUT DIED VERY YOUNG

Emanuel Collins

Had restless Time, whose harvest is each
  hour,
Paus'd but a while, and gaz'd upon this
  Flower :
In pity he had turn'd his scythe away,
And left it blooming to a distant day ;
But ruthless he mow'd on, and this, alas !
Too soon fell with'ring with the common
  grass.

ON MY FIRST DAUGHTER

Ben Jonson

Here lies, to each her parent's ruth,
Mary, the daughter of their youth ;
Yet all heaven's gifts being heaven's due,
It makes the father less to rue.
At six months' end, she parted hence
With safety of her innocence ;
Whose soul heaven's Queen, whose name
  she bears,
In comfort of her mother's tears,
Hath plac'd amongst her virgin-train :
Where while that severed doth remain,
This grave partakes the fleshly birth ;
Which cover lightly, gentle earth !

UPON A MAID
Robert Herrick

Here she lies (in bed of spice)
Fair as Eve in Paradise :
For her beauty it was such
Poets could not praise too much.
Virgins come, and in a Ring
Her supremest requiem sing ;
Then depart, but see ye tread
Lightly, lightly o'er the dead.

ON THE LITTLE REGINA COLLIER
Catherine Philips

Virtue's blossom, Beauty's bud,
The pride of all that's fair and good,
By Death's fierce hand was snatchèd hence
In her state of Innocence :
Who by it this advantage gains,
Her wages got without her pains.

ON A CHILD
Thomas Gray

Here freed from pain, secure from misery, lies
A Child, the darling of his parent's eyes ;
A gentler lamb ne'er sported on the plain,
A fairer flower will never bloom again !
Few were the days allotted to his breath ;
Here let him sleep in peace his night of
    death.

ON MISTRESS ANNE KNYVETON

Thomas Bancroft

Here hidden lies dear treasure under ground,
Blest innocence, with budding virtue
    crowned,
That, like a taper on some altar fired,
Shone fairly forth, and sweetly so expired,
Expecting here, in darksome shade of night,
A rising Sun, that brings eternal light.

ON ELEANOR FREEMAN, WHO DIED A.D. 1650, AGED 21

From Select Beauties of Ancient English Poetry, 1787

A virgin blossom in her May
Of youth and virtues turned to clay ;
Rich earth accomplish'd with those graces
That adorn Saints in heavenly places.
Let not Death boast his conquering power—
She'll rise a Star, that fell a Flower.

OCCASION'D BY THE DEATH OF A YOUNG GIRL

Josiah Relph : from Martial

Censure no more the hand of Death,
That stopp'd so early Stella's breath ;
Nor let an easy error be
Charged with the name of cruelty :
He heard her sense, her virtues told,
And took her—well he might—for old.

ON A VIRGIN DYING FOR LOVE
Samuel Sheppard

Ye virgins that this tomb pass by,
Behold the same with weeping eye,
Accuse the blind god of stern wrath,
That he this virgin here laid hath ;
For he was partial—nothing mov'd
He wounded her, not him she lov'd.

EPITAPH
Lady Margaret Sackville

My beauty was
  So fine and fair,
You'd think it woven
  Out of air.

All full of colour
  And of sun—
How like a breath
  Of air 'tis gone !

ON THE DEATH OF A FINE GIRL
AT NINE YEARS OLD
Richard Graves

Joy of her friends ; her parents' only pride ;
When scarce she'd tasted life, Clarissa died.
She was—but words are wanting to say what:
Say all that's good and pretty—she was that.

UPON A WOMAN AND HER CHILD, BURIED IN THE SAME GRAVE

George Wither

Beneath this marble stone doth lie
The subject of Death's tyranny—
A mother, who in this close tomb
Sleeps with the issue of her womb.
Though cruelly inclin'd was he,
And with the fruit shook down the tree,
Yet was his cruelty in vain,
For tree and fruit shall spring again.

ON A VERY YOUNG LADY

Brian Edwards

Scarce had the tender hand of Time
    Maria's bloom brought forth,
Nor yet advanc'd to Beauty's prime,
    Tho' ripe in Beauty's worth :

When Fate untimely seal'd her doom
    And shew'd, in one short hour,
A lovely sky, an envious gloom,
    A rainbow and a show'r.

ON ELIZABETH THOMAS
Ob. 1808, Aet 27

From Pettigrew's Epitaphs, 1857

She'd no fault save what travellers give the
    moon :
Her light was lovely, but she died too soon.

ON HIS DAUGHTER RACHEL, WHO DIED ON HER FATHER'S BIRTHDAY

Henry Carey

That fatal day, which lent my earliest breath,
Gave my dear girl to the cold arms of Death:
Others in triumph may their birthday keep;
Mine calls aloud for tears, and bids me weep.

ON THE DEATH OF A SCOTCH NOBLEMAN

William Drummond

Fame, register of Time,
Write in thy scroll, that I
Of wisdom lover, and sweet poesy,
Was cropped in my prime :
And ripe in worth, though green in years
    did die.

ON MISTRESS JOANNA BYRON

From A Curious Collection of Epitaphs, 1727

Admir'd, belov'd, lamented infancy,
Hurry'd away, does here untimely lie,
Too good to live, and yet too young to die :
Hard Fate! that best of things must be
Always the plunder of the grave and thee.
What grief can vent this loss, or praises tell
How young, how good, how beautiful she fell?
Complete in all but days, resign'd her breath,
Who never disobey'd but in her death.

ON ONE NAMELESS
Walter de la Mare

Blessed Mary, pity me,
Who was a Virgin too, like thee ;
But had, please God, no little son
To shower a lifetime's sorrows on.

IN OBITUM M.S., X° MAIJ, 1614
William Browne

May ! Be thou never grac'd with birds that
    sing,
        Nor Flora's pride !
In thee all flowers and roses spring.
        Mine only died.

ON —— , BORN BEFORE HIS TIME
From Wit's Recreations, 1640

Griev'd at the world and times, this early
    bloom
Look'd round and sigh'd, and stole into his
    tomb.
His fall was like his birth, too quick ; this
    rose
Made haste to spread, and the same haste to
    close :
Here lies his dust, but his best tomb's fled
    hence,
For marble cannot last like innocence.

A MONUMENT
(AFTER AN ANCIENT FASHION)

I. A. Williams

Traveller, turn a mournful eye
Where my lady's ashes lie ;
If thou hast a sweet thine own
Pity me, that am alone ;—
Yet, if thou no lover be,
Nor hast been, I'll pity thee.

TO THE MEMORY OF THE VIRTUOUS
GENTLEWOMAN, RACHELL
LINDSAY

William Drummond

The daughter of a king of princely parts,
In beauty eminent, in virtues chief,
Loadstar of love, and loadstone of all hearts,
Her friends' and husband's only joy, now
    grief,
    Enclosèd lies within this narrow grave,
    Whose paragon no times, no climates have.

ON DAME ETHELDRED REYNELL

From A Curious Collection of Epitaphs, 1727

Modest, humble, godly, wise,
Pity ever in her eyes,
Patience ever in her breast ;
Great in good, in evil least :
Loving wife, and mother dear,
Such she was that now lies here.

ON ELIZABETH L. H.
Ben Jonson

Would'st thou hear what man can say
    In a little ? Reader, stay.
Underneath this stone doth lie
    As much beauty as could die :
Which in life did harbour give
    To more virtue than doth live.
If at all she had a fault,
    Leave it buried in this vault.
One name was *Elizabeth*,
    The other, let it sleep with death :
Fitter, where it died, to tell,
    Than that it lived at all. Farewell !

ON ANNE BURTON
From Toldervy's Epitaphs, 1755

Reader, stand back ; dull not this marble
    shrine,
With irreligious breath : the stone's divine,
And does enclose a wonder—Beauty, Wit,
Devotion, and Virginity with it.
Which, like a lilly fainting in its prime,
Wither'd and left the world ; deceitful Time
Cropt it too soon : and Earth, the self-same
    womb
From whence it sprung, is now become the
    tomb.
Whose sweeter soul, a flower of matchless
    price,
Transplanted is from hence to Paradise.

l

TO ROBIN REDBREAST
Robert Herrick

Laid out for dead, let thy last kindness be
With leaves and moss-work for to cover me :
And while the wood-nymphs my cold corpse
    inter,
Sing thou my dirge, sweet warbling choris-
    ter !
For epitaph, in foliage next write this—
Here, here the tomb of Robin Herrick is.

AD MUSAM SUAM
DE OBITU FORTISSIMI INSIGNISQUE IUVENIS THOMAE
EGERTON MILITIS
John Weever

Descend my Muse into the bed of Death,
(Embalming first his body with thy tears)
And chide the Fates until they lend him
    breath,
Because they rapt him in his youthful years ;
Yet stay my Muse, Fates offered him no
    wrong,
In virtue old he was, in years though young.

ON A SOLDIER
From Wit's Recreations, 1640

When I was young, in Wars I shed my blood
Both for my King and for my Country's good :
In elder years my care was chief to be
Soldier to Him that shed His Blood for me.

ON MRS. MARTHA PALMER, 1617
From A Curious Collection of Epitaphs, 1727
Can Man be silent and not praises find,
For her who lived the praise of woman-kind,
Whose outward frame was lent the world to
    guess
What shapes our souls shall wear in happi-
    ness,
Whose virtue did all ill so oversway
That her whole life was a Communion day.

ON THE DEATH OF SIR ALBERTUS
    AND LADY MORTON
      Sir Henry Wotton
He first deceas'd—she, for a little, try'd
To live without him, lik'd it not and dy'd.

ON MISTRESS MARGARET PASTON
    OF BARNINGHAM, NORFOLK
      John Dryden
So fair, so young, so innocent, so sweet,
So ripe a judgment and so rare a wit,
Require at least an age in one to meet ;
In her they met ; but long they could not
    stay,
'Twas gold too fine to mix without allay.
Heav'n's image was in her so well express'd,
Her very sight upbraided all the rest :
Too justly ravish'd from an age like this,
Now she is gone, the world is of a piece.

NED VAUGHAN
Walter de la Mare

A Shepherd, Ned Vaughan,
'Neath this Tombstone do bide,
His Crook in his hand,
And his Dog him beside.
Bleak and cold fell the Snow
On Marchmallysdon Steep,
And folded both sheepdog
And Shepherd in Sleep.

ON A PARISH CLERK
William Shenstone

Here lies, within this tomb, so calm,
Old Giles ; pray sound his knell :
Who thought no song was like a psalm,
No music like a bell.

ON A PARISH CLERK
From Frobisher's Epitaphs, circa 1800

Here lies entomb'd within this vault so dark,
A Taylor, Cloth-Drawer, Soldier, and a
Clerk.
Death snatch'd him hence, and also from
him took
His Needle, Thimble, Sword, and Prayer
Book ;
He could no longer work, nor fight, what
then ?
He left the World, and faintly cry'd—*Amen.*

SAM CHEALE
L. A. G. Strong

Here lies Sam Cheale, a quiet man
  Whose whistle was his only pride,
Which same he played uncommon well.
  We have no music since he died.

AT BERKELEY, GLOUCESTERSHIRE
Jonathan Swift

Here lies the Earl of Suffolk's fool,
  Men called him Dicky Pearce ;
His folly served to make folks laugh,
  When wit and mirth were scarce.

Poor Dick, alas ! is dead and gone,
  What signifies to cry ?
Dickies enough are still behind,
  To laugh at by and by.

ON TOM D'URFEY
From Lewis's First Miscellany, 1726

Here lies the Lyric, who with tale and song
Did life to three-score years and ten prolong :
His tale was pleasant and his song was sweet ;
His heart was cheerful—but his thirst was
    great.
Grieve, reader, grieve, that he too soon
    grown old,
His song has ended and his tale has told.

ON A FOOTMAN
John Heath

This nimble footman ran away from Death,
And here he rested, being out of breath ;
Here Death him overtook, made him his
    slave,
And sent him on an errand to the grave.

ON ALEXANDER LAYTON,
MASTER OF DEFENCE, 1679
From Hackett's Epitaphs, 1757

His thrusts like lightning flew ; but skilful
    Death
Parry'd 'em all, and put him out of breath.

ON DAVID FLETCHER, SMITH,
DIED 1744
From the Christmas Treat, 1767*

My sledge and hammer lie reclin'd,
My bellows, too, have lost their wind ;
My fire's extinguished ; forge decayed ;
And in the dust my vice is laid ;
My coal is spent ; my iron gone ;
My last nail's driven, my work is done.

---

* A common folk epitaph. It occurs in *A Collection of Epigrams*, 2nd edition, Vol, II, 1737, with two additional lines.

    My fire-dried corpse lies here at rest,
    My soul, smoke-like, is soaring to be blest.

ON A SCHOLAR
From Wit's Recreations, 1640

Forbear, friend, t' unclasp this book ;
Only in the forefront look,
For in it have errors been,
Which made the author call it in :
   Yet know this, 't shall have more worth,
   At the second coming forth.

ON ALEXANDER ROLLE, GENT.,
1660
From A Curious Collection of Epitaphs, 1727

Under this marble lies a treasure,
   Which Earth hath lost and Heaven gain'd,
Wherein we mortals took great pleasure,
   Whilst his blest soul on Earth remain'd :
     A lawyer, yet desir'd to see
     His client's right more than his fee.

ON A YOUNG WOMAN
From Wit's Recreations, 1640

The body which within this earth is laid,
Twice six weeks knew a wife, a saint, a maid;
Fair maid, chaste wife, pure saint, yet 'tis
   not strange
She was a woman, therefore pleas'd to change :
And now she's dead, some woman doth
   remain,
For still she hopes once to be chang'd again.

QUARTERS

From Norfolk's Epitaphs, 1861

Billeted here by death
In quarters I remain ;
When the last trumpet sounds,
I'll rise and march again.

ON CAPTAIN JOHN DUNCH

From A Curious Collection of Epitaphs, 1727

Though Boreas' blasts and Neptune's
    waves
    Have tossed me to and fro,
In spite of both, by God's decree,
    I harbour here below,
Where I do now at anchor ride,
    With many of our fleet,—
Yet once again I must set sail,
    Our admiral Christ to meet.

ON SIR FRANCIS DRAKE DROWNED

From Wit's Recreations, 1640

Where Drake first found, there last he lost
    his fame :
And for a tomb left nothing but his name.
His body's buried under some great wave,
The Sea that was his glory, is his grave :
Of him no man true epitaph can make,
For who can say, Here lies Sir Francis
    Drake ?

ON SIR FRANCIS VERE, 1608
From Camden's Remains, 1623

When Vere sought death, arm'd with his
    sword and shield,
Death was afraid to meet him in the field ;
But when his weapon he had laid aside,
Death, like a coward, struck him, and he died.

UPON ONE WHO DIED IN
PRISON

From Wit's Recreations, 1640

Reader, I liv'd, enquire no more,
Lest a spy enter in at door ;
Such are the times, a dead man dare
Not trust nor credit common air.
But die and lie entombèd here,
By me,—I'll whisper in thine ear
Such things as only dust to dust
(And without witness) may entrust.

IN THE WALL OF STEPNEY CHURCH
From A Curious Collection of Epitaphs, 1727

Of Carthage great I was a stone ;
O mortals, read with pity !
Time consumes all, it spareth none,
Man, mountain, town nor city ;
Therefore, O mortals all, bethink
You, whereunto *you* must—
Since now such stately buildings do
Lie buried in the dust.

ON LORD DANVERS

George Herbert

Sacred marble, safely keep
His dust who under thee must sleep,
Until the graves again restore
Their dead, and Time shall be no more.
Mean while, if He which all things wears
Do ruin thee, or if the tears
Are shed for him dissolve thy frame,
Thou art requited ; for his fame,
His virtues, and his worth shall be
Another monument for thee.

IN THE CHURCH OF ST. PETER AND ST. PAUL IN CANTERBURY

(An inscription on a marble in the North Porch,
where seven Archbishops of Canterbury were buried,
viz., Augustine the first, Laurentius, Mellitus, Justus,
Honorius, Deusdedit and Theodosius.)

From A Curious Collection of Epitaphs, 1727

Of England Primates seven, and Patriarchs
    seven,
Seven Governors, seven Labourers in
    Heaven,
Seven Wells of Endless Life, Seven Candles
    Light,
Seven Palms of this our Land, seven Dia-
    dems bright,
Seven shining Stars, this vaulted floor con
    tains.

ON HIS WIFE

William Browne

Thou need'st no tomb (my wife) for thou
    hast one,
To which all marble is as pumix-stone.
Thou art engrav'd so deeply in my heart,
It shall outlast the strongest hand of art.
Death shall not blot thee thence, although I
    must
In all my other parts dissolve to dust ;
For thy dear name, thy happy memory,
May so embalm it for eternity,
That when I rise, the name of my dear wife
Shall there be seen, as in the book of life.

ON HIS MISTRESS' DEATH

From Wit's Recreations, 1640

Unjustly we complain of Fate,
For short'ning our unhappy days,
When death doth nothing but translate,
And print us in a better phrase.
Yet who can choose but weep ? not I :
That beauty of such excellence,
And more virtue than could die,
By death's rude hand is vanish'd hence.
Sleep, blest creature, in thine urn,
My sighs, my tears, shall not awake thee.
I but stay until my turn ;
And then, O then ! I'll overtake thee.

ON MR. HUGH MARCHANT, 1714

From A Curious Collection of Epitaphs, 1727

When, by Inclemency of Air,
These golden Letters disappear,
And Time's old canker'd Teeth have shown
Their Malice on this Marble Stone,
Virtue and Art shall write his Name
In Annals, and consign his Fame
To Monuments more lasting far
Than Marble Stones or Golden Letters are.

ON THE COUNTESS DOWAGER OF
PEMBROKE

William Browne

Underneath this sable hearse
Lies the subject of all verse :
Sidney's sister, Pembroke's mother :
Death, ere thou hast slain another
Fair, and learn'd, and good as she,
Time shall throw a dart at thee.

Marble piles let no man raise
To her name : for after days
Some kind woman born as she,
Reading this, like Niobe
Shall turn marble, and become
Both her mourner and her tomb.

AN EPITAPH
Walter de la Mare

Here lies a most beautiful lady,
Light of step and heart was she ;
I think she was the most beautiful lady
That ever was in the West Country.
But beauty vanishes ; beauty passes ;
However rare—rare it be ;
And when I crumble, who will remember
This lady of the West Country ?

AGE
William Lisle Bowles

Age, thou the loss of health and friends
shalt mourn !
But thou art passing to that night-still
bourne,
Where labour sleeps. The linnet, chattering
loud
To the May morn, shall sing ; thou, in thy
shroud,
Forgetful and forgotten, sink to rest ;
And grass-green be the sod upon thy breast !

MY OWN EPITAPH
George Darley

Mortal, pass on !—leave me my desolate
home !
I care not for thy sigh ; I scorn thy tear ;
To this wild spot let no intruder come,
The winds and rains of Heaven alone
shall mourn me here !

ON ETHELBURGA, QUEEN OF THE
WEST SAXONS

From A Curious Collection of Epitaphs, 1727*

I was, I am not ; smil'd, that since did
    weep ;
Labour'd, that rest ; I wak'd, that now must
    sleep :
I play'd, I play not ; sung, that now am still:
Saw, that am blind; I would, that have no
    will.
I fed, that now feed worms ; I stood, I fell :
I bade God save you, that now bid farewell.
I felt, I feel not ; follow'd, was pursued :
I war'd, have peace ; I conquer'd, am sub-
    dued.
I mov'd, want motion ; I was stiff, that bow
Below the earth ; then something, nothing
    now.
I catch'd, am caught ; I travel'd, here I lie ;
Liv'd in the world, that to the world now
    die.

* I have made some slight amendments, obviously
needed by the text.

Finding rough but similar lines, as a translation
from " Textor," in Timothy Kendall's *Flowers of
Epigrammes*, 1577, I consulted Dr. F. P. Barnard, and
with his help traced the following too closely-woven
Latin epitaph by " Ravisius Textor " (Jean Tixier
de Ravisy, 1470 ?-1524 ?), as the original of this fine
poem :

EPITAPHIUM

Risi, ploro : fui, non sum : studui, requiesco :
Lusi, non ludo : cecini, nunc muteo : pavi
Corpus, alo vermes : vigilavi, dormio : dixi

ON ROBERT CRYTOFT, DIED 1810

From Notes and Queries, 15th March, 1854

As I walk'd by myself, I talk'd to myself,
    And thus myself said to me ;
Look to thyself, and take care of thyself,
    For nobody cares for thee.
So I turned to myself, and I answered myself
    In the self-same reverie,
Look to myself, or look not to myself,
    The self-same thing it will be.

ON THE LADY CALENDAR

From A Curious Collection of Epitaphs, 1727

Here lies the Phœnix of her sex, the ark
Where loyalty and honour did embark,
The day of our deluge ; what, had She been,
Had She been He, a soul so masculine !
Bruce, Wallace, should remounted have the
        stage
Of action, with the worthiest of that age.
She was a Woman (I'll not shame Men much),
But had our lords and leaders all been such,
Our King and Country 'd not been sold by
        knaves,
Nor should we now go supplicate like slaves.

Salve, dico vale : rapui, rapior : superavi,
Vincor : certavi, pace utor, jure ego vixi,
Jure igitur morior : non obsto, obstare nequirem.
Terra fui quondam, rursus sum terra, nihil sum.
Terra caduca vale, vermes, salvete, recumbo.

ON A SOLDIER
Margaret Postgate

Ask me not whether he were friend or foe
    That lies beneath,
Nor whether in a worthy fight or no
    He came to death.
Pass on, and leave such reckonings unmoved,
    Remembering now
Here lieth one who gave for that he loved
    A greater gift than thou.

EPITAPH ON HIMSELF
Sir Thomas Overbury

Now measur'd out my days, 'tis here I rest,
That is, my body ; but my soul his guest
Is hence ascended, whither neither Time,
Nor Faith, nor Hope, but only Love can
    climb :
Where being now enlightened she doth know
The truth of all things which are talk'd
    below :
    Only this dust doth here in pawn remain,
    That, when the world dissolves, shall*
      come again.

* I think I am justified in this emendation for
" she'll." A parallel is provided by the epitaph on
Mrs. Martha Palmer (page 147), an alternative version
of which has—for its fourth line—" What shapes our
souls she'll wear in happiness."

ON MICHAEL DRAYTON, ESQ.

Ben Jonson

Do, pious marble, let thy readers know
What they, and what their children owe
To Drayton's name ; whose sacred dust
We recommend unto thy trust.
Protect his memory, and preserve his story,
Remain a lasting monument of his glory.—
And when thy ruins shall disclaim
To be the treasurer of his name ;
His name, that cannot die, shall be
An everlasting monument to thee.

ON THE DEATH OF LADY ARABELLA STUART*

Richard Corbet

How do I thank thee, Death, and bless thy
      power,
That I have past the guard, and 'scaped the
      Tower !
And now my pardon is my epitaph,
And a small coffin my poor carcass hath ;
For at thy charge both soul and body were
Enlarg'd at last, secur'd from hope and fear.
That among saints, this amongst kings is laid ;
And what my birth did claim, my death hath
      paid.

* She was imprisoned in the Tower for some years.
She died in 1615 and was buried in Westminster
Abbey.

ON THE DUKE OF BUCKINGHAM
James Shirley

Here lies the best and worst of fate,
Two kings' delight, the people's hate,
The courtier's star, the kingdom's eye,
A man to draw an angel by,
 Fear's despiser, Villiers' glory,
 The great man's volume, all time's story.

ON THE PORTRAIT OF SHAKESPEARE
WRITTEN UNDER MARTIN DROUESHOUT'S ENGRAVING IN THE 1ST EDITION OF THE PLAYS
Ben Jonson

This figure that thou here seest put,
It was for gentle Shakespeare cut,
Wherein the graver had a strife
With nature, to outdo the life :
O could he but have drawn his wit
As well in brass, as he has hit
His face ; the print would then surpass
All that was ever writ in brass :
But since he cannot, reader, look
Not on his picture, but his book.

TO SIR JOHN ROE
Ben Jonson

I'll not offend thee with a vain tear more,
Glad-mention'd Roe ; thou art but gone
 before,
Whither the world must follow : and I, now

Breathe to expect my *When*, and make my
    How.
Which if most gracious heaven grant like
    thin e,
Who wets my grave, can be no friend of mine.

ON MR. FRANCIS BEAUMONT
Richard Corbet

He that hath such acuteness and such wit,
As would ask ten good heads to husband it :
He, that can write so well that no man dare
Refuse it for the best, let him beware :
    Beaumont is dead, by whose sole death
        appears,
    Wit's a disease consumes men in few
        years.

ON THE EARL OF DUNDEE
John Dryden : from the Latin of Dr. Pitcairn

Oh last and best of Scots ! who didst main-
    tain
Thy country's freedom from a foreign reign.
New people fill the land now thou art gone,
New Gods the temples, and new kings the
    throne.
Scotland and thou did each in other live,
Nor wouldst thou her, nor could she thee
    survive.
Farewell ! who dying did support the State,
And couldst not fall but with thy country's
    fate.

ON THE DEATH OF KING CHARLES I
The Marquis of Montrose : written with the
point of his sword

Great ! Good ! and Just ! Could I but rate
My griefs, and thy too rigid fate,
I'd weep the world to such a strain,
As it should deluge once again.
But since thy loud-tongu'd blood demands
    supplies
More from Briareus' hands than Argus' eyes,
I'll sing thy obsequies with trumpet sounds,
And write thy epitaph with blood and
    wounds.

TO THE MEMORY OF THAT LOYAL
  PATRIOT, SIR I. CORDEL, KT.
          Alexander Brome

Thus fell the grace and glory of our time,
Who durst be good when goodness was a
    crime ;
A magistrate that justly wore his gown
While England had a king, or king a crown ;
But stoutly flung it off, when once he saw
Might knock down Right, and Lust did
    justle Law.
His soul scorn'd a democracy, and would
No longer stay, than while the kingdom
    stood ;
  And when that fled, his follow'd it, to be
  Join'd to his king i' th' hieromonarchy.

ON EPICTETUS, THE SLAVE

C : from the Greek

Want's bitter path I, Epictetus, trod ;
A slave and cripple—yet beloved of God.

ON MR. ROBERT PORT

Charles Cotton

Here lies he whom the Tyrant's rage
Snatcht in a venerable age ;
And here, with him, intomb'd do lie
Honour, and Hospitality.

CHALKHILL

**FROM HIS LATIN EPITAPH IN THE CLOISTERS OF
WINCHESTER COLLEGE**

Lionel Johnson

Here lies John Chalkhill : years two score
A Fellow here, and then no more !
Long life, of chaste and sober mood,
Of silence and of solitude ;
Of plenteous alms, of plenteous prayer,
Of sanctity and inward care :
So lived the Church's early fold,
So saintly anchorites of old.
A little child, he did begin
The Heaven of Heavens by storm to win :
At eighty years he entered in.

UPON A CHAMBER-MAID DECEASED

*Thomas Pecke : from the Latin of
Sir Thomas More*

Her body served : her soul was always free.
Kind Death hath set that too at liberty.

ON A HUSBAND AND WIFE

P. J. Foley

They were so one, that none could say
Which of them rul'd, or whether did obey—
He ruled, because she would obey ; and she,
In so obeying, rul'd as well as he.

ON CLUER DICEY

Hannah More

O thou, or friend or stranger, who shalt tread
These solemn mansions of the silent dead,
Think, when this record to enquiring eyes
No more shall tell the spot where Dicey lies ;
When this frail marble, faithless to its trust,
Mould'ring itself, resigns his moulder'd dust ;
When time shall fail, and nature feel decay,
And earth, and sun, and skies, dissolve away ;
The soul this consummation shall survive,
Defy the wreck, and but begin to live :
Oh pause ! reflect, repent, resolve, amend !
Life has no length—Eternity no end.

ON A MAN AND HIS WIFE

From Lewis's First Miscellany, 1726

Here sleep, whom neither life, nor love,
  Nor friendship's strictest tie
Could in such close embrace as thou,
  Thou faithful grave, ally.

Preserve them, each dissolv'd in each,
  For bands of love divine,
For union only more complete,
  Thou faithful grave, than thine.

ON MRS. CORBET

WHO DIED AFTER A LONG AND PAINFUL SICKNESS,
1ST MARCH, 1724

Alexander Pope

Here rests a woman good without pretence,
Blest with plain reason, and with sober
    sense ;
No conquest she, but o'er herself, desir'd,
No arts essay'd, but not to be admir'd.
Passion and Pride were to her soul unknown,
Convinc'd that Virtue only is our own.
So unaffected, so compos'd a mind ;
So firm, yet soft ; so strong, yet so refin'd ;
Heav'n, as its purest gold, by tortures try'd !
The Saint sustain'd it, but the Woman dy'd.

ON ADMIRAL BLAKE
From A Curious Collection of Epitaphs, 1727

Here lies a man made Spain and Holland
 shake,
Made France to tremble, and the Turks to
 quake ;
Thus he tam'd men, but if a lady stood
In 's sight, it raised a palsy in his blood ;
Cupid's antagonist, who in his life
Had fortune as familiar as a wife.
A stiff, hard, iron soldier ; for he
It seems had more of Mars than Mercury ;
At sea he thunder'd, calm'd each raging
 wave,
And now he's dead, sent thundering to his
 grave.

ON JOE MILLER
Stephen Duck

If humour, wit, and honesty could save
The hum'rous, witty, honest from the grave ;
The grave had not so soon this tenant found,
Whom honesty, and wit, and humour
 crowned.
Or could esteem and love preserve our
 breath,
And guard us longer from the stroke of
 death,
The stroke of death on him had later fell,
Whom all mankind esteem'd and lov'd so
 well.

ON THE DEATH OF MR. AIKMAN

James Thomson

As those we love decay, we die in part ;
String after string is sever'd from the heart,
Till loosen'd life, at last, but breathing clay,
Without one pang is glad to fall away.

Unhappy he who latest feels the blow,
Whose eyes have wept o'er every friend laid
        low,
Dragg'd ling'ring on from partial death to
        death,
Till, dying, all he can resign is breath.

FOR HOGARTH'S MONUMENT IN CHISWICK CHURCHYARD

David Garrick

Farewell, great painter of mankind,
    Who reach'd the noblest point of art ;
Whose pictur'd morals charm the mind,
    And through the eye correct the heart !

If genius fire thee, reader, stay ;
    If nature touch thee, drop a tear :—
If neither move thee, turn away,
    For Hogarth's honour'd dust lies here.

AFTER MONS
Shane Leslie

We lie like castaways upon the shore
   Whose lives were lost upon the Great
    Retreat,
But whither ebb hath been, the flow shall
    pour,
   And we await the tide's returning feet.

AS AT THERMOPYLAE
Shane Leslie

Stranger, since we could but die—
   If the English have not heard,
Tell them that their soldiers lie
   Here, obedient to their word.

EPITAPH ON AN ARMY OF MERCENARIES
A. E. Housman

These, in the day when Heaven was falling,
   The hour when Earth's foundation fled,
Followed their mercenary calling
   And took their wages and are dead.

Their shoulders held the sky suspended ;
   They stood, and Earth's foundations stay ;
What God abandoned, these defended
   And saved the sum of things for pay.

ON A WIFE
Francis Coutts

Once I learnt in wilful hour
How to vex him ; still I keep,
Now unwilfully, my power :
Every day he comes to weep.

ON A FOOL
Francis Coutts

Stranger, stay ! yet shed no tear ;
For a fool lies buried here ;
Yet, since he unfinished lies,
God in time may make him wise.

ON THE DEATH OF EDWARD FORBES
Sydney Dobell

Nature, a jealous mistress, laid him low.
He woo'd and won her ; and, by love made
    bold,
She showed him more than mortal man
    should know,
Then slew him lest her secret should be told.

EPITAPH
Lady Margaret Sackville

Why did you die ?—I died of everything.
    Life was deep waters robbing me of breath,
Sorrow, delight, love, music, Winter, Spring,
    Slew me in turn—and last of all came
    Death.

ON ROBERT AIKEN

Robert Burns

Know thou, O stranger to the fame
Of this much lov'd, much honour'd name,
(For none that knew him need be told)
A warmer heart Death ne'er made cold.

ON LADY CAROLINE MAXSE

George Meredith

To them that knew her, there is vital flame
In these the simple letters of her name,
To them that knew her not, be it but said,
So strong a spirit is not of the dead.

EPITAPH

Aubrey de Vere

From Youth's soft haunt she passed to Love's
 fair nest ;—
Thence on to larger Love and heavenlier
 rest :
Four years their sunshine, two their shadows
 lent
To enrich a heart with either lot content.
Pray well, pure Spirit ! and some sad grace
 accord
To him once more thy suppliant ; once thy
 lord.

EPITAPH FOR HIMSELF

S. T. Coleridge

Stop, Christian passer-by !—stop, child of
    God,
And read with gentle breast. Beneath this
    sod
A poet lies, or that which once seem'd he.—
O, lift one thought in prayer for S. T. C. ;
That he who many a year with toil of breath
Found death in life, may here find life in
    death !
Mercy for praise—to be forgiven for fame
He ask'd, and hoped, through Christ. Do
    thou the same !

EPITAPH

Thomas Hardy

I never cared for Life : Life cared for me,
And hence I owed it some fidelity.
It now says, " Cease ; at length thou hast
    learnt to grind
Sufficient toll for an unwilling mind,
And I dismiss thee—not without regard
That thou didst ask no ill-advised reward,
Nor sought in me much more than thou
    couldst find."

EPITAPH FOR HIMSELF

From Paul Scarron : Dodd's Epigrammatists,

1870

Tread softly ; make no noise
    To break his slumbers deep ;
Poor Scarron here enjoys   ·
    His first calm night of sleep.

VERSES BEFORE DEATH

Sir Walter Raleigh

Even such is time, that takes in trust
    Our youth, our joys, our all we have,
And pays us but with earth and dust ;
    Who, in the dark and silent grave,
When we have wandered all our ways,
Shuts up the story of our days ;
But from this earth, this grave, this dust,
My God shall raise me up, I trust !

INDEX OF FIRST LINES

175

192